T0194227

A Path Of Light

Alba Ambert

iUniverse, Inc.
Bloomington

A Path Of Light

iUniverse books may be ordered through booksellers or by contacting:

iUniverse
1663 Liberty Drive
Bloomington, IN 47403
www.iuniverse.com
1-800-Authors (1-800-288-4677)

Because of the dynamic nature of the Internet, any web addresses or links contained in this book may have changed since publication and may no longer be valid.

Any people depicted in stock imagery provided by Thinkstock are models, and such images are being used for illustrative purposes only.

Certain stock imagery © Thinkstock.

Cover photograph by Baron Laurent de Posson.
Cover design by Yanira Ambert.

ISBN: 978-1-4620-0255-9 (sc)
ISBN: 978-1-4620-0256-6 (ebk)

Printed in the United States of America

iUniverse rev. date: 5/9/2011

Contents

Prologue vii

Awakening 1

Purification 12

Transcendence 30

Surrender 56

Union 68

Epilogue 80

About the Author 83

About the Paramita Path 84

Paramita Path Centers 89

Prologue

There is a spark in your soul that is aware of the Creator's presence within itself. It is astonishing that we do not perceive the Creator's presence within us when this presence is closer to us than we are to ourselves. Our spiritual evolution depends on this awareness, the awareness of the Creator's presence inside each one of us. When we recognize this awareness it transforms our perspective of life, of reality, of everything else. For then we know that just as the Creator's presence is in us, it is also in the rock, the cow and the person beside us.

The Path of Light discussed in these pages brings you to this awareness, an awareness that is very simple and accessible to each one of us. It requires a journey into your heart where you find that in the deepest core of your being is the immutable presence of God, our Creator[1]. You realize that God has always been there, closer to you

---

1   Creator, God, the All-That-Is or the Divine Presence will be used interchangeably to designate the Supreme Being who is, in reality, Nameless.

than your own breath. There is nothing to do, or be, or say, or think. There is nothing to seek. It is there and the only way to realize this is through Love. In this way, the path of Light is the path of Love. Love will bring you Home. It is the Way.

This path is a radiant Light that sparkles in the heart and ignites the most joyful, unimaginable Love. When it is felt in the deepest, most sacred space of the heart, you realize that this is the Creator's Love, that the Light that shimmers and glows within you is a sacred reflection of divine Love. The Love and the Light are the same. The path of Light is the path of Love. The path of Love is the path of Light. Love light, light love, it is all one wondrous journey into the heart. The culmination of this journey is often called enlightenment or union with God.

Though no one can bring you into the Beloved's heart, for this is a journey each one of us embarks on our own, I have asked the Creator to guide me to the Truth so that I may remind you of it and to guide my hand and my heart as I write these words so that I may perhaps offer you a map that when followed can show you the way into a place of Light you already know, but have forgotten. It is not the only map to the Divine heart, but it is the map I charted on my own journey into the Light. In this map, I indicate the wide boulevards to freedom as well as the pitfalls, those narrow alleys that obstruct our view of the sacred path with dark mazes and seemingly impenetrable walls.

The map can be easy to follow or make your journey hard to endure, depending on what you make of the challenges of your life. Your life's purpose, after all, is to make this journey into the Light. You have returned to this world lifetime after lifetime to reach your ultimate destination, to return to the Creator's embrace, to return Home. Accept your soul's purpose with joy and the journey, though not effortless, will be smoother to navigate.

I hope you will accept the lamp I am holding before you, illuminating the map, illuminating the path, casting aside the stones, brushing away the dust and pointing the way until you reach the great chasm of trust. Then, it is up to you either to cling to the roots of a tree that will hold you firmly on the ground of unknowingness or make the leap into the spacious luminosity of surrender where Divine Love is the only reward.

In this book I discuss the five transformative stages of union with the Creator as I experienced them in my own mystical journey to union with God. These stages are awakening, purification, transcendence, surrender and union. I call the journey toward union the Path of Light. I find it useful to describe this Path of Light as a beautiful quartz pyramid with its wide base firmly planted in the ground and its Light-filled apex soaring into the sky. During our lives we exist in the periphery of this pyramid. Then one day we awaken to the realization that there is more to life than the physical. Our heart breaks with longing for something beyond ourselves and at that moment of realization, a gate opens into the base of the pyramid. This is the part that lies on the Earth and is closest to the physical aspects of our selves. Through the gate at the base of the pyramid we enter into the first chamber. This represents the beginning of our journey. The chamber at the base of the pyramid is wide and filled with other souls, activities and objects. It is prone to distract us. Although the quartz pyramid is almost transparent and through your inner eye you should be able to see the intricate patterns of light coming from it and enjoy the crystalline structure of the quartz glittering from its surface and around it; your eyes are still filled with the dust of the outside and you cannot see clearly the beauty of where you are. On many occasions while in this chamber, you will turn away from the radiant vistas offered by the pyramid's light and seek distractions in the darker areas of the chamber.

Once you are ready, your heart will guide you to look upwards and notice that there is a spiral staircase leading to the higher chambers of the pyramid. The staircase curves round and round as it ascends and it seems to reach up to the sky. But at this initial stage of the journey you cannot see the apex of the pyramid, the fifth and last chamber that soars above you high into the unknown reaches of the spiritual realms. The apex is where you touch the radiant point of light that brings you to union with the Creator. There are luminous bridges of colored lights that span the many chambers on each level of the glimmering pyramid. In the facets of the quartz you will one day see pyramids inside pyramids inside pyramids, to infinity. And there will be a time when you will feel the vibration of the quartz pyramid, a vibration of harmony, of peace, of love. This vibration will raise you to the most radiant planes of Light.

The symbol of the pyramid is a visual guide to help you navigate through the Path of Light. The chambers may at times connect to one another, or dip downward before ascending to a higher plane. These chambers do not necessarily occur sequentially. It is possible for two or even three levels to be experienced side by side, or aspects of one chamber to be present in another chamber. Nor do the chambers need to be ascended in the order in which I present them. Some may appear earlier or later in your spiritual journey to Oneness. There is also no way to determine the amount of time in which you will dwell in each chamber. You may reside in a chamber for months yet remain in another for years or even decades. Even when you reach the apex of the pyramid where your soul unites with God, the truth is that the path toward union with the Creator is a lifelong journey. Full and absolute union occurs when we are completely free of the physical body. Then, our soul is released and we become pure spirit within the heart of God.

This is not the first time we have been at a similar juncture in time and space; a crossroad where the Light beckoned from behind a cloud. On those occasions and now, I have come to show you the map, offer reminders, bring you to the brink of timeless awareness. It has been my mission in many lifetimes to gather you together and point the way. Your soul remembers me and perhaps other parts of you remember the voice, remember the words, remember the beauty of the promise. As in all the previous lifetimes when we journeyed together, I ask you again to trust the Light that the Creator is showing you, surrender your being to the Light and everything will be taken care of.

We are poised here at the rim of time. Before us is an expanse of timeless Light, beauty, peace, harmony and joy. Behind us is the time-laden density of the world of illusion, the unreal stage we have created to live out our lessons on Earth. You have the opportunity now, at this moment, to turn towards the radiant planes of Light and step into them joyfully, fearlessly and with open arms. Intend, right now, to cut all attachments that deaden your hopes and force you to shove your feet into shoes of lead. Intend to step into the Light.

It is your choice now to open your heart and allow the Light, in all of its splendor, to stream through every particle of your being, transforming everything within you and outside of your self. Or you can remain in your leaden shoes, imprisoned in the cage of your attachments, desires and drama.

This is your chance. Choose to set yourself free. Choose to bring down the bars of your prison. Choose to soar with the Light. To be free, all you have to do is intend for the Light to enter the sacredness of who you are and allow it to stream through you in all its magnificent spaciousness and luminosity. Then you surrender to the Light, surrender to the Creator.

Many miracles will manifest when you turn to the Light. Be ready for them and welcome them into your life without doubt, without fear. Expect transformations, not only in yourself and how you relate to others and to the world, but also in your surroundings. Some changes will be unexpected, but they will be exactly what you need to reach enlightenment in this lifetime.

At this moment we are witnessing the end of the old and the beginning of a new era. We are letting go of the old density and welcoming the elevated vibrations of the Light. It is important that you let go of everything that keeps you tied to the old and with an open and free heart walk into the new Light.

I invite you to enjoy the Grace that this Light brings to your life, to embrace the Love with which this gift has been generously bestowed upon you and to be grateful to the Creator and all the beings of Light who are guiding you.

This is the moment, the time is now to become One with the Beloved. In an exquisite dance of Love, the lover and the Beloved unite for all eternity.

May your journey be tender and Love-filled. May you walk in the Light.

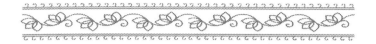

Awakening

I was born with a wound in my heart. The wound was a longing that burrowed deeply into my being, like a subterranean river. And wherever I lived, wherever I breathed, I felt like a stranger and the world became a cold, unfriendly place. I searched for meaning through the passageways of the intellect, the alleys of relationships, the convoluted avenues of distractions and drama. Yet the wound was there, like an unfriendly presence. My mistake, a common one, was searching for the balm that would heal my heart outside of myself.

One night, in the darkness of my room the walls seemed to push against my chest. I felt utterly alone, abandoned, forsaken. I called out to the heavens but there was only silence. So I called out again and again, until my throat was sandpaper and my eyes stitched closed. I had never known such sorrow. I don't know how long this torment lasted, for time became an eternal cry in the night of my soul that stretched out into an endless desert.

And in the midst of this desolation, a tiny light flickered in my heart.

And I cried out to the light, "I will not die in this terrible desert of loneliness and longing! I want to live, I want to live in you, in the light." And the tiny seed of light burst and blossomed in my heart. It became liquid and swelled and overflowed.

That's when the Creator came to my heart, a vision of beauty I could never attempt to describe. My knees gave way and I crumbled like a rag. I was so tiny, a drop of water in an infinite ocean of Love. In the Light I recognized the Love of the Creator, the true nature of Reality. I understood that the Creator is Love, and the Creator is All. The world, the universe, all existence changed at that moment. As I surfaced from that intense moment of despair when the Creator seemed to have abandoned me and all of creation, I realized with wonder and gratitude that a veil had lifted. The Creator was not gone; the Creator was within me so close I was incapable until that moment of sensing the beautiful Presence. With a flash of recognition I realized that the boundaries had collapsed, the veil dropped and I was a being transformed by the touch of God on my heart.

At that instant of realization, I was moved to perform a simple ceremony. I prepared a small altar with candles and incense and made a solemn vow. I dedicated my life to the Creator and promised to do whatever he[2] wanted me to do. At this point, an internal conversation between

2   The Creator is our Mother and our Father, our infinite Source who contains all within Itself. I use the masculine pronoun throughout this book for the sake of expediency and with the understanding that God is neither masculine nor feminine. God Is.

my soul and the Creator began and I opened my heart to divine guidance.

The moment of awakening is like opening your eyes after a deep sleep. You catch a glimpse of the Light –which can last an instant but the effects will be with you for a day or several days—and you see that the reality you have been living is false. You see the true Reality, the Reality of the Creator's Love, which is a higher plane of existence that is Light-drenched and beautiful. You understand that you were looking for the Creator under tables, behind closed doors, inside suitcases. It can be compared to being in a dark room thinking you were alone until you hear something that sounds like a man clearing his throat and then you realize that someone else is there, though you cannot see him. Like the man in the dark room, the Creator is present but we aren't aware of his presence. We believe we are alone and insist on looking for him elsewhere. We cannot look for the Creator outside of ourselves, just as it wouldn't occur to us to look for our arm inside our bedroom closet in the morning. How can you imagine the Creator anywhere else, but in you? The Creator and you are One. If you look for the Creator outside of yourself, you will never find him. You must go beyond the idea of the Creator, the idea of truth and go to the beginning of all beginnings, to the origin, the source of all goodness and of all truth and this is the Creator. You find him in your heart.

As our search for meaning intensifies, we ask ourselves: Who are we? Why are we here? What is the purpose of life, of death? In our attempt to make sense of the world, we use our brain, but as we reside in this chamber of the pyramid we realize that the brain is fraught with limitations. The harder we attempt to find answers, the more evident it becomes that logical explanations acceptable to the mind are beyond its purview. For the brain, though powerful, remains a physical organ that will perish when we die with the rest of our physical self. Deep inside we suspect that there is more to what we are than our brain can indicate or even know and we search for answers beyond the rational world. Very often when we turn to extra-intellectual realms, the sacred texts of our religions provide no satisfactory answers either. Something inside us, a stirring perhaps, the wisp of a memory we cannot quite remember or experiences that are logically inexplicable, alert us to other, truer possibilities.

This reality that is beyond the reality of the senses, is revealed to us often unexpectedly. One night my husband Walter and I were driving back home from another city. We had recently moved to the area and were not very familiar with the capillary of roads and highways circling our town. It was a moonless night and we were unable to see the street signs clearly. After driving through unfamiliar territory for some time we wound up on a hill. At a distance we caught a glimpse of the highway that would take us home, but we were on the opposite side of the highway. We pondered on how we could get to the other side. What happened next is difficult to explain because it occurred in an interval of "no time," a trans-spatial, trans-temporal dimension. We slipped, or cut through the membrane of time/space. Without realizing how it happened we found ourselves driving down the opposite side of the highway from where we were, exactly where we wanted to be. We looked at each other and

Walter said: "How did that happen?" I shook my head and said nothing, knowing that we had transcended the membrane in space and time that separates us from other dimensions. We did so without trying. Our desire to get on the road leading us home was so great that in a moment of infinite Grace, the Creator put us there and we were on our way.

Many logically unexplainable incidents like this occur in all our lives. Then we realize that existence certainly is not limited to the physical aspects perceived by our senses; that our beingness expands beyond our physical body and the projections of the mind. We recognize in our hearts that we have been given, through no effort of our own, an unexpected gift of Grace. This is when we often begin to delve deeply into the spiritual configurations of existence. We develop an intense feeling of separateness and hunger for a spiritual union with our Source, but have no inkling as to the origin of this longing. We often turn to philosophy, to the musings of men and women of great intellects, until we realize that they have not found the answers either. This stage in our journey to Source is often a period of seeking. We embark on a quest to find a map, a teacher, a discipline that will bring us fully into the fulfillment of our life's purpose. It is important to seek, but it is equally important to find a spiritual path as soon as possible and stay on it. Otherwise you risk the danger of being a seeker always and distracted by the quest, you will remain in the chamber at the base of the pyramid and never realize the true purpose of your soul.

The stage of awakening constitutes the first chamber in the quartz pyramid. You walk through the gate and you finally understand the many times that God has called to your heart, either in dreams or even in nightmares that attempt to rouse you to your inner truth. You may have felt the tug at your heart when you were moved to tears by the beauty of words, or nature, or art. There was a moment when God called to me with such force that I still remember every detail of that invitation.

One spring, Walter and I were driving from Burgundy to Lake Como and we stopped in Monaco for a couple of days. After lunch, we took a walk through the steep narrow streets of an old neighborhood in Monte Carlo. As in a dream we heard beautiful music that streamed through the stillness of the afternoon. We followed the music to a centuries-old church. The intricately carved doors were open. We entered and sat at one of the pews. The church was empty except for the organist who was rehearsing Bach's Toccata and Fugue in D Minor. I'll never forget it. Although I had heard the composition many times, I had never heard it played by an angel. The notes echoed through the high ceilings of the church, soared through the statues of saints, and rested firmly in my heart. I closed my eyes and was transported to the higher realms of Light as the waves of the music washed through my being and carried me onward, higher and higher, until I was no longer in my body. I had no sense of my surroundings. Thoughts stopped completely and I soared like the wind into the Light. Then the soaring stopped and my soul rested at a place I could not describe at the time. It was a place of infinite peace. My heart opened and all I felt was Love.

I didn't really feel the Love. Rather, the Love was the only reality that existed and I was part of it. Now that I have a deeper awareness of the spiritual realms, I know that the music was a call from the Creator to guide me Home. The experience lasted less than five minutes, I would imagine, since the Bach composition is only about seven or eight minutes long. But I knew at that moment that something monumental had happened and the core of my being was affected forever. It was unfortunate that after only a few days the experience was relegated by my mind to the background. But although the mind tried to forget, my soul was indelibly etched by this insistent call from the Beloved.

You may have had experiences such as the one I describe. It is quite common at this stage to find yourself called by God through music, nature, poetry or something as delicate and ineffable as watching an infant sleep. In an instant you find yourself transported to a higher realm and experience a heightened state of consciousness. And still, we may not have responded to the call. It is at these times, when we are deaf to the call, that a heavy blow such as an illness or the loss of a loved one or very dark nightmares may force us to reverse our misguided course and begin our journey into the Light.

At some point in your life, after a gentle tug to your heart or a forceful shake that affects the very foundation of your life, you may decide to heed the call of Spirit. As you decide to fulfill your soul's true purpose and enter through the gate, you are launched fully into a path of spiritual evolution, a path into the Light. Almost everyone has entered this initial chamber and had moments of awakening. The difficulty is that we live this moment of awakening and do not move beyond it. We let it pass as if it were a chance occurrence that does not belong in our daily existence and we walk out through the gate once more. We return to our state of forgetting. It is also possible to believe that this is it; that a realization of this nature is enlightenment and there is nothing else to attain. This may be one of the most common errors in the spiritual path since the stage of awakening to the Reality of the Creator is only the beginning. It is only the entryway into the crystalline pyramid and there is much work to be done beyond this first stage. Awakening to the Light is the onset of a long journey that lasts a lifetime.

The experience of awakening, of entering into the first chamber of the quartz pyramid, can be described as a re-birth into the Light. We start at the beginning, knowing full well that there is no beginning, nor end, only an endless flow of infinity, an endless birthing into life, into Light.

The child of God is born continuously every time a soul inhabits a physical body and God, the Creator, breathes life into it. With each birth God creates a divine child of Light to seed the physical with his Light. We are seeds of Light sent here to furrow the Earth into paths and plant these seeds in lines of Light that crisscross the firmament with divine energy. Every one of us, as the Creator's child, has the potential of a Buddha or a Jesus or a Shankara to bring the divine Light into the world.

So it is that the Creator comes into us every moment. It is what is meant in the gender-specific terms of the Bible by the phrase "begetting a Son." And it is done again and again. Every instant, the birth of the Creator's divine child is occurring and it is happening in each one of us. We need to be aware of this.

The Creator ceaselessly begets you as his divine child. You spring from this sacred seed of Light and there is no distinction between you and the Creator. You are one. You are his only divine child and in you is every divine child that has ever been born and who shall ever be in the eternity of the Creator's acts. Once you are born as his divine child, you want or need nothing from the Creator, for you have it all.

Your birth as a divine child is always happening and it is happening in you and in everyone and everything. This is the potential of Oneness that we all have. This is the potential of union. However, even in this stage of awakening, we are not always conscious of it.

And where does this birth occur? Where does this potential exist within us to be born, as God's children of Light, again and again? How does this happen? It happens through the birth of the Creator's Love in our hearts. At the moment of awakening, divine Love is born within us with the Creator's Light and Will.

The Light is the song in your heart that rises to the heights of unimaginable beauty when you recognize who you are. However, at the stage of awakening we are often not fully conscious of the Light in our hearts. Many receive this Light, bask in its splendor for a moment, but the pull of the ego drives them back into the density of the false reality. The first chamber of the pyramid is spacious and offers many opportunities for distraction and forgetfulness and it is very easy to walk out through the gate and into the world of density once more. The Light is so strong at times that the ego resists more than ever, sensing its imminent demise, and you may be pushed away from the Light.

At this time of awakening, when you are still unsure of what is happening to you and may be tempted to continue to heed the call of the ego, it is crucial to make a choice, a choice that will determine your survival as a divine child. You have entered a vast chamber, flooded with Light, your eyes half-closed by the dust you collected in the outside world of the senses. Choose to open your heart and allow the Light, in all its magnificence, to stream through every molecule of your being, removing the dust from your eyes so you may see, transforming everything within you and without. Then, you will have the opportunity to mature as God's child and fulfill your potential as a divine instrument of Light.

If at this stage you choose to return to the world of the senses, the material world where the ego reclaims you with its enticements, you will remain stuck in your leaden shoes; imprisoned in the cage of your attachments, desires and drama. You can choose to walk back out, shut the gate of liberation behind you and return to the density of the world where you will once more forget the Light in your heart.

But if you choose to stay in the pyramid, you will be greatly rewarded. Through strong determination and intention, you can decide to dedicate your life to fulfilling your soul's purpose, maturing as a divine child, entering into the Creator's Love in your heart. At this stage you will begin your spiritual practice in earnest, praying and meditating, listening to guidance from the higher planes, receiving spiritual messages in your dreams and enjoying the awareness of the infinite, eternal Light in your heart. Soon you realize that this Light is the Creator's Love. Then you are ready to make a commitment to live completely in the radiance of his Love, in the beauty of his Light. Once you have chosen God as your priority, you are ready to ascend the steps of the quartz pyramid and enter into the second chamber, the chamber of purification.

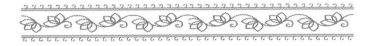

Purification

As the blindingly beautiful Light illuminated my soul, the moment of rapturous wonder passed and I saw the darkness inside my heart. At the time, I was not aware that the dark curtain shrouding my being was the ego. I was only aware of its ugliness and the suffering it caused me when I meditated or prayed and thoughts or emotions would spring out of nowhere to interrupt my spiritual practice. I was struck by my own unworthiness. How was it possible that I, who had made so many mistakes in life, often behaved badly and taken so many wrong turns could aspire to union with God's Love? How could I even contemplate the possibility of divine grace? Was my awakening a fluke, a great mistake or worse, a cosmic joke?

But still, I looked above me and saw the spiral staircase leading upwards and my soul urged me to climb to the next chamber of the pyramid. During this time, I was struck by the need to be pure so that I could deserve the great gift of Light that I was now fully aware of. Later, I would understand that God's Love is given freely and has nothing to do with deserving or merit or earning. The only requirement is within our own hearts. We are the ones who must make the necessary adjustments in our lives and open our hearts so that divine Love can flow through, purify us and make us whole. The Love is there. You simply need to open your heart to receive it.

I entered the second chamber of the pyramid when I understood my urgent need for spiritual purification. Purification is the process in which –through awareness and effort– you begin to open your heart and dissolve the blockages and obstacles of the ego that prevent you from reaching union with the Creator. The purification stage is, perhaps, the most difficult and lengthy in the journey to union with God. Purification is what makes every subsequent step possible.

Purification entails the removal, cleansing and releasing of attachments, blockages, negativity and ego domination at the physical, mental, emotional and spiritual levels so that the Light of God's Love may shine through us. Purification brings purity to the soul and the heart and the clarity to see the Truth of who we are. Through spiritual purification we begin to integrate our consciousness with the unity of God. Purification erases all else that is not Love within ourselves so we may fulfill our purpose as God's children bringing Love into the world.

One of my first spiritual purification experiences consisted of walking on fire, a symbolic act that held within itself an important key to my liberation. I attended a weekend workshop on something that had to do with freedom of the self. Right now I cannot remember much about the workshop, not even the title. All I remember is the firewalking event that was held on the last day of the workshop as a dramatic finale. That evening, to the cadence of drums and the flickering light of candles, I walked barefoot on a twelve-foot long glowing bed of red-hot coals. Although the temperature of the blazing coals was 1,500 degrees Fahrenheit, I walked on the embers unharmed.

I experienced this firewalk at the very beginning of my spiritual journey when many uncertainties loomed before me. I doubted my own strength to pursue a path that I knew would change my life in profound, irreversible ways. Walking on fire was transforming. It lifted me to new heights and allowed me to be aware of the strength and courage in my heart. If I could walk on fire, I could do anything. The fire of that walk burnt through my fears, insecurities and doubts. Great inner peace followed in its wake. It was a propitious start to working with the ego because I realized that even something as hard as the ego could be vanquished, if I was determined to do so. It is not necessary, of course, to walk on fire to understand the strength of your being. Your ability to overcome fears and take control of your destiny is evident once you open your heart to the perfection of God's Love.

At the time of my awakening, I was living in England and the opportunity arose to attend a spiritual retreat in Wales. When the train pulled into the solitary station at Abergavenny, I knew at once that the sparkling emerald green meadows and hills, the slow pace of living and the silence of the ancient rock formations would be a perfect backdrop for the difficult interior work I would do that week. In the silence of the retreat, my meditation practice extended for what seemed like eons and I dove into a deep reflection of my inner self. There, I confronted the attachments, judgments, emotions and other negative ties that held me prisoner and unable to see the self I truly was. I realized that my awakening to the Light was not enough because it had been a flicker in the darkness and did not last. Rather, it was necessary that I purify my being to be able to turn to the Creator completely, immersed in the reality of his Love, without any distractions. This required eliminating all the elements of the false reality not in harmony with the Light. The false reality, I realized, was an inferior reflection of the true Reality of the Creator's Love.

In an instant of realization I understood that I was not in the presence of the Creator for one reason alone: my ego's control. I knew that I had to remain alert to the distractions the ego set up in front of me. Before doing anything or being with anyone I began to ask myself: "Does this person or activity bring me closer to the Creator or does it distance me from the Divine Presence?" I suggest that you too question all your actions and the persons you spend time with. This simple question will help you be in the moment, aware of the Creator's presence, and will automatically turn you towards the divinity in your heart.

I knew I had to give up everything that kept me bound and separate from God; all that kept me unaware of his presence in my heart. Some things were easy to renounce, such as the material objects that didn't matter to me very much or habits that were not deeply rooted. Harder to release were my attachments to my books, friendships, opinions, fixed beliefs, pastimes; and everything else that

I considered valuable until I understood that the Creator is all that matters.

Certain activities, persons, behaviors, emotions, traits, patterns of conduct and material things were an obstacle to my union with the Creator. No matter how pleasurable, they constituted a wall that obstructed my view of God's Light. When I became vigilant and paid attention to those people, activities, behaviors and other things in my life that distanced me from my spiritual practice, that distracted me from being in the presence of my Beloved, I knew I had to get rid of them. These were obstacles that nurtured and strengthened my ego, so it became essential to remove them from my life as a first step in dissolving the ego and the illusory reality it created with false thoughts, negative emotions and denial of the truth. As long as I believed that these were part of my true self, I could not be free to discover the truth of my being. I pledged to do whatever was necessary to die to myself so that my true being could be born in the Light.

Attachments to our children and other loved ones are the most difficult to dissolve. We think that trying to control others proves our love for them and that we do so for their own good. We disapprove of actions or decisions that are not in accordance with what we believe is best for them and convince ourselves that by attempting to block these, we are demonstrating love. Yet, true love is unconditional and it is not based on the behaviors or decisions of our loved ones. When we love without expectations, without trying to control, without any desire for others to comply with our wishes or unrealized desires; our love is the source of great joy. When we love and only love, there are no cords, attachments or ties from the ego. When we truly love, our love blossoms from the heart and we accept our loved ones just as they are without trying to change them or manipulate them or create a false dependency. When we love without attachments, our love is pure and free. This is the love that springs from the freedom of an open heart.

Although some of the biggest obstacles to my freedom were the physical, mental and emotional attachments that bound me tightly to the false reality of the ego, I soon realized that I also had spiritual attachments that I needed to wipe out. It is sometimes difficult to believe that our spiritual practices can become attachments, yet this is a pitfall we must avoid on the path to union with God. Being attached to "enlightenment" or to "spiritual evolution" is as much a tie that binds us as an attachment to a house, a habit or a person.

At the Wales retreat, I became painfully aware of my personality and how this personality defined me. My name, my profession, my place of birth were all parts of who I thought I was. I am a professor. My name is Alba. I am Puerto Rican. Yet none of that is who I really am. Those are just impermanent aspects of my illusory self. In a past life, I may have been a sailor named Tariq, living in Alexandria. "Who am I, truly?" I asked myself. That question was the necessary first step in discovering the true nature of my being.

By ego I do not refer to the Freudian ego that is the organized part of the personality. The ego, as discussed in this book, is the mistaken idea you have of who/what you are[3]. The ego causes a sense of separation, of abandonment

---

3   For more information on the ego, please see my book, *The Seven Powers of Spiritual Evolution.*

by the Creator. It is based on fear. The ego is that part of ourselves that deludes us into believing that we are separate from the Creator, from others and from the rest of reality. The ego's only interest is to keep itself alive, strong and dominant by driving us further away from union with the Creator. Union causes the dissolution of the ego and the ego will do anything to avoid its own destruction.

The ego is the cause of all suffering in the world and this suffering is unnecessary. Most human beings are imprisoned in the cage of their ego and dominated by the ego's most powerful instruments: the mind and emotions. The domination of the ego blocks our ability to listen to our hearts. While the illusory reality of the ego exerts its dominion, our spiritual heart remains closed and we are unable to access the wisdom and truth of our heart. It is only by opening the heart and realizing the truth within that we will find peace in our selves and project it to the world. To do this, we must deal with the challenges of the ego that distract us with useless reasoning, drama, doubt, fear and attachments. One of the most distinct challenges in our path to union with the Creator is the barrier created by our ego that does not allow us to remember who we are.

The ego binds us to three things that prevent us from being one with the Creator. The first is time, the second is physical matter, and the third is complexity.

1. Time. We are bound to the passing of time, the notion that we live within an inexorable movement of days and nights and years and decades. Worried and distracted as we are by this movement that is enthralling and

hypnotizing, we focus on what has passed, dwelling on events that are no longer there. Or we focus on a future that we can only assume will happen. Yet we have no way of knowing that the future will materialize. While we fret about the past and worry about the future, the present moment —which is all that really exists— escapes through the frozen planes of the past and future. The past and the future, our preoccupation at all times, are unreal. The real is the present moment and it passes through without our notice.

The Creator is timeless. The Creator is beyond the artificial construct of time. To attain union with the Creator we must remain in the moment.

2. Physical matter binds us with its density. We are physically bound to the material world and to our senses, which we mistakenly believe are detectors of truth. We rely on the material world –a limited three-dimensional extent in which we move and where events occur with relative position and direction—for all our information on who and what we are and where we are. Yet, there is an inner dimension of the spiritual planes that is vast, eternal and infinite which we do not explore, tied as we are to the finitude of the material aspects of our lives.

To attain union with the Creator, we need to transcend physical matter, reach inwards to the vastness of our being and there, beyond the three dimensional limitation of form, we discover that he has always been there.

3. Complexity is another aspect of the ego that keeps us away from God. The ego causes us to be mired in complexity, complication and a maze of apparent difficulties. We complicate our lives with issues, problems and distorted thinking and find ourselves needing these complications and believing that the multiple is superior to the simple. Yet, the Creator is not found in the multiplicity of things, but in the unity of all. You need to realize that you are not a separate being. You are One with all that is, a part of the whole of existence. There is only One and to attain union with the Creator, the many must be made one in you.

   Simplicity is an important key to your spiritual evolution. God-consciousness is simple, Love is simple, remaining in your heart is simple. It is only the ego's attempt to keep us in servitude that makes us believe that union with God is complex, that divine Love is difficult to attain. The complexities of the mind unravel when confronted with the simplicity that God is.

Once we are freed from the constraints of time, physical matter and complexity we are free to see the truth of the Creator and of our being.

Upon awakening, the false world my ego had constructed flashed before me. Behind its darkness, sparkling like the sun, was the immensity of the Light. When I saw myself in the radiance of that Light, I realized that whatever stood in the way of being in that Light needed to go. I knew then that I was imprisoned by the ego and I longed to be free to exist in that Light always. A deep yearning stirred in my heart to rest in the Beloved Creator's sweet embrace. I had never known such longing and I was determined to cleanse myself of all desires, all needs and wants. The only longing that exists, I knew then, is longing for the Creator. All other longing, all other desire is ego-derived and therefore false. What was required was a complete annihilation of the self, casting off all that held me down until my heart was empty of everything. In this emptiness I knew I could transcend the world of illusion and attain consciousness of the Creator's loving Presence.

But, how can we purify ourselves so we may attain this gift of grace? What can we do, if anything, to attain the consciousness of God's Love within our hearts? Is there something we can do to allow the divine in our souls to be present? Just as the ground is prepared for sowing by pulling out weeds, fertilizing the soil, loosening clumps and removing stones, in the same manner our souls and hearts require the proper readiness for our rebirth into Light.

For this to occur your ego must be tamed, your emotions curbed, your thoughts held in check so that the silence necessary for the resonance of the Creator's Love can come through. You turn inward to the presence of the Creator, live in the moment and quell your desires for anything. In the nothingness of your being, your heart shines through and touches God. Then, God enters and you are reborn as a divine child. At that moment, the Creator's Love is indelibly etched in your heart, in your soul, in the core of your being. Love becomes the essence of your existence, of all existence.

There is the physical you and the spiritual you. The physical you is ego-bound, dominated by the mind, the emotions and fear. The spiritual you is heart-centered, infused with love, eager to fulfill your soul's purpose and filled with love of God. The spiritual aspect of your self takes pleasure in its connection with the Creator, loving the self and others and limiting its being as a physical self to that which is necessary to devote your material existence to the Creator's will.

Many people waste their time in the physical manifestation following the ego's false directions, bent on living in the world of illusion that is far removed from the Creator's Light. It is a dense world of specters and shadows that does not move them into the reality of spirit that is the true Reality.

In this way, many people live their entire lives like Plato's prisoners in the cave. In the Allegory of the Cave, Plato describes prisoners who have lived in a cave since childhood. Tightly bound by chains at the legs and necks, they cannot turn their heads. All they see is a wall in front of them. Behind the prisoners, a fire blazes. Between the fire and the prisoners there is a stand where puppeteers walk. The puppeteers are behind the prisoners and hold up different objects that are reflected as shadows on the wall. This is all that the chained prisoners see: their own shadows, the shadows of their companions and the objects projected on the wall. Instead of seeing the real objects and real persons, the prisoners see mere shadows of the objects and persons yet believe that what they see is real.

Plato used this allegory to teach that most of us consider reality to be what we name it, not the true form that is behind its designation. So when we say the word "feather," we believe that the superficial aspects of it, the illusion of it, is its true nature, rather than the form that constitutes its underlying reality. Beyond the physical world, Plato taught, are ideal forms. These ideal forms are the true reality. According to Plato, the philosopher is like a prisoner released from the cave; able to understand that the shadows on the wall are an illusion and, therefore, able to perceive the form that underlies the physical world. This form constitutes the true reality.

One could easily use Plato's myth of the cave to illustrate the illusion in which most people live, bound as they are by the chains of the ego. As we live in a cave, prisoners of our ego, we can only see shadows of the Real. A shadow of the Real is not real, it is an illusion and we can easily slip into a life of illusion believing that the false reality presented by our egos is the true Reality of the Creator's Love. As we liberate ourselves from ego-domination and are able to live outside the cave of illusion, we realize the nature of true Reality that is the truth of our spiritual self

You can bring down the veils of illusion created by the ego by consciously being aware of the Creator's presence in your life; by living your life in the true Reality of the Creator's Love and Light. It doesn't mean that you will never feel pain, or grief, or worry. This would be impossible as long as you are in a physical body that has a neurological formation, a cellular structure, a hormonal system and everything else that makes us physical beings. What this means is that you feel pain, grief, worry, anger and you realize that this is not who you are.

You are not what you experience. Therefore, you should not identify with your emotions. You observe your experience and surrender it to the Creator. You let it go and by letting it go you are free to enjoy the peace and love that you truly are.

As the layers of ego dissolved like sugar granules in a bowl of water, I reached a state of desirelessness where I rested in emptiness, in nothingness. This emptiness is where I met God in all of his splendor because there was nothing else inside me except him and only he could fill me completely. Through him I transcended desires, emotions, wanting, striving. Through him I surrendered all of my attachments – including the most difficult attachment to my only daughter– without reservations, without doubts, expecting nothing in return. Through this desirelessness, born of surrender, I realized that my family is humanity and my home is the world and that every time I love another, I love the Creator because the Creator is everything.

Then, only then, as I emptied myself of everything else, empty until I reached the point of nothingness, was I ready for God to communicate and act through me. It is like taking a piece of paper to write a letter. If the paper is filled with doodles, script, drawings, you cannot write on it. To be able to write, you need a paper that is blank. So it is that the Creator can communicate with us when our heart is empty of everything else, but him. Empty yourself out so that you may know God.

We live most of our days distracted by the ego-dominated world. The part of us that is filled with God remains hidden and we are not aware of his presence. In this state, we cannot access the Love that is there to offer us refuge. Divine Light is hidden behind the dense veil our ego sets up so we cannot awaken from our dream. And our hearts remain closed. Yet even those people whose hearts are closed to the awareness of God, talk about him as if they knew him. To know the Creator is to know him beyond the constraints of the ego. The person who enjoys talking about the Creator and invoking the Creator but has not surrendered to the divine presence, does not know him. To know the Creator is to move beyond words, beyond thoughts, beyond emotions and rest in the stillness of his presence. This stillness is beyond space and time, beyond thoughts and words and requires that we die to ourselves so that we can be born again in the Creator's Light.

Although it may seem hard to die to everything, to be as a desert, to annihilate the self in order to find the Creator, it is truly simple to do for the Creator is there already within you. It is you who are far from the Creator. The Creator is within and you are outside. Allow the door of your heart to open. Walk in without hesitation or fear. The Creator is waiting. Allow the Creator to live in your heart and then you will realize that within the Creator you are more alive, more vibrant, more Light-filled and joyous than you had ever been in the dim reality of the material world.

In this emptying out of yourself, you become transparent and more Light can come through you. Work with the Light by calling it to you, by intending for the Light to fill you completely. You will find that the purity of the Light cleanses and purifies everything. If you allow it, the Light pushes everything that is not Love away from you. And as you allow this to happen, you are filled with infinite peace. Desirelessness and emptiness result in true awareness of God –without the encumbrances, burdens and limitations of the physical self— and union with God is possible.

But you must be willing to let go of everything else, so your heart is pure and only the Love of the Creator can dwell in your heart. The Creator hides nothing from a pure heart. A pure heart is one devoid of desire, filled only with love and devotion to the Creator. As your love for the Creator fills you completely, you dissolve in the Love and you are One with the Love.

When your heart is pure, turned toward the Creator at all times, it is a sparkling vessel where the Creator's Love manifests. This cannot happen if you are so preoccupied by the material world, the distractions of the senses, the domination of the ego that your soul is marginalized and spends most of its time in the higher realms waiting for you to turn toward God. The soul is the spark of God within your heart and it links you to the divine, but you need to be aware of your soul so it may guide you to divinity.

As I attempted to scale the wall of obstacles that kept me imprisoned and hidden from the Light, I had a number of dreams and wakeful experiences in which I remembered traumas from past lives. These were similar to visions, except they were not radiantly Light-filled, as visions are, but shared a quality of dimness (like reality in the physical world). As the past lives claimed my attention, I recognized patterns of hurt, connections to persons in my current lifetime that had an origin in past lifetimes and even physical illnesses and conditions that were rooted in other lives. I realized then the burdens we carry from lifetime to lifetime and the need to heal the karma accumulated. We collect karma over our many reincarnations. Accumulated karma creates blockages in our energy channels and these blockages prevent us from attaining God-consciousness. It is imperative that we clear karma, both from past and present lifetimes, so that we may progress spiritually.

Karmic healing is part of the purification process that clears our energy bodies and allows us to bring in the Light. It is impossible to know everything we have experienced throughout all our incarnations. However, once you have done a substantial amount of karmic healing, recognized your mistakes and surrendered whatever you don't know about your past to God; an act of Grace occurs and the Love of the Creator's Light dissolves all karma in an instant. This gift of Grace is usually granted in the fourth stage of the Path of Light when you have completely surrendered to the Creator.

The spiritual practice of purification allows you to turn to God without hindrances. You remove the obstacles and blockages that impede the full flow of the Light into your being by following a disciplined practice[4]. This involves an awareness of the life force energy that exists throughout

---

4   In my book, *The Seven Powers of Spiritual Evolution,* I discuss
     spiritual practices that assist the purification process.

your body and the ability to keep this energy flowing freely. Purification requires stilling the mind and bringing silence into your being through prayer, meditation and the conscious cultivation of silence in your daily life. You purify yourself by doing good, living an ethical life, letting go of attachments and by forgiving. In spiritual purification you let go of the karmic loads that burden your being. You begin the ego dissolution that is necessary to open your heart to the Light of the Creator's Love and to reach union with your Source.

Once God knocks at your heart as he did that night when the Light pierced through my eyes and settled in my heart, it is important to heed the call. It is a gentle knock at first, like a twig tapping at a window. Distracted by our beehive lives, we often don't hear the gentle tap; we can't feel the tug at the heart. Then the knock becomes stronger, more forceful, and we raise our head and wonder: "Who is that knocking at my heart?" And we breathe in desolation.

The desolation you feel is the result of a longing in your heart for the Creator's Love. When St. John of the Cross wrote about the dark night of the soul, he was describing the hole that exists in your heart when you feel a sense a separation from the Creator and from the rest of existence. Through the spiritual practice of purification you can resolve this longing in your heart by emptying yourself completely and allowing the Creator's Light to fill you.

The second chamber of the pyramid, the room of purification, is a difficult one that involves ego dissolution, desirelessness and emptying yourself of everything but your love and devotion to the Creator. It is a stage in which you move closer to a harmonized calibration of your desires so that you only want what is in accordance with the Creator's Will. Many persons spend years and even decades in this very important stage in their spiritual journey. It is possible to move on to a higher chamber, only to return to the chamber of purification for additional work. The process can be greatly accelerated by determination, effort and a focused desire to move forward into the Light. In order to reach the next chamber, that of transcendence, your heart must recognize that the purpose of your soul is to return to God and everything else in your life becomes a means to propel you Home.

Transcendence

In the morning I sit at the sunroom sipping my first glass of water of the day. I place a hand over the glass and radiate the water intending to fill it with Light. My hands become pulsating hearts, warm and incandescent. The water molecules, impregnated with Light, suffused with love and gratitude, transmute into a luminous substance that I know can heal. Transmutation of water into Light, I am ready to drink. The well-water splashes my palate and tongue awakening trillions of tiny buds that savor and discern. Judgment is immediate: The water is delicious. It slips easily down my throat and settles in the stomach from where I envision the Light-charged water drifting like a river through the atoms in my body, igniting each cell like candles. I am a breathing, candle-lit cathedral of Light. I drink some more and the Light expands like a galaxy, past the skin and into my aura until everything shimmers and I cannot distinguish myself from the Light. And in this state of absolute oneness, with eyes that glow like lanterns, I look through the huge panes of glass to the woods that encircle my house like the arms of a lover.

At a distance, the property dips into a narrow gorge and rises once more to meet the road. At the far wall of the gorge, pine trees and shrubs scramble for space and sunlight. Then I see shadows dancing in the sun-dappled woods. Could they be nymphs, devas or other nature spirits? I wonder. Gradually, I discern a shape that drifts between the pines, its dusky movement, calm and graceful, blending with the bark of pines. My eyes adjust and I can see a head, a body, and then another and another until the herd of deer emerges from the mist, chewing on berries, stopping suddenly as deer do when they are startled by a noise or when they sense movement. Then they clamber down the sloping wall, the fawns lingering behind the does, distracted by leaves and squirrels and scents of the unseen.

There, in that morning tableaux, I am lost in the eternal moment. I have been gently painted into the landscape by a benevolent artist. I am one with the green of the leaves, the gentle sigh of the wind, the cautious step of the deer. A deep realization rises, like a sun in my heart. I have been wounded by not having known this oneness for so long, by believing in the religion of separation, my wounds scarred over by the lonely yearning for what was lost. And now, in this infinite moment that opens like a thousand universes; the taste of water, the deer, the pine trees, the sunlit sky, all gather me into themselves. I am sheltered in a cocoon of Light where I fuse and dissolve and become what I have always been: one with all. The wound has been healed and I am whole.

After the initial awakening and purification, the chamber of transcendence is a very beautiful stage of love and joy in your journey toward union with the Creator. You have climbed the spiral stairs and reached the third chamber. You have passed the halfway mark. In this phase of your journey, you go beyond your physical reality, understand the false world of the ego and experience transcendence, that is, an awareness of God's Love, a God-consciousness that is all-encompassing, abiding, always present. You cultivate silence and it becomes a much-desired sacrament, a sacred ritual that allows you to dwell in God-awareness at all times. In this phase of your spiritual journey, you open your heart completely to the Creator's Love, to the Creator's Light.

Love is the main theme of transcendence. In this stage you love everyone you know, everyone you see, everyone you think of. You look at others with a love that comes from the deepest recesses of your heart. You see God in the eyes of others, aware of the divine spark within them, and you love God in them. Later, in the stage of union you will love only God, and through your love of God you will love others; you will love them in God. That is, your love of God which is the only love you will be capable of feeling, will spill out of your heart and touch everyone you know, everyone you meet, all of existence and all who dwell in existence. In the stage of transcendence, though, you will love God in others rather than loving others in God.

A warning is necessary here. Because of the bliss, ecstasy, profound love, and possibly spiritual visions and revelations that you might experience during this period, it is easily conceived as the end of the journey. However, transcendence is a turning point, a critical one that will lead you to the most important stages that follow. It is essential to recognize that union with the Creator is still to come and requires a full, deep and complete surrender of your being. In the meantime, the period of transcendence is to be enjoyed. It is a luminous time of fulfillment and joy to be relished without forgetting that it is not the end of the journey.

There was once a time when we lived connected to our instincts, to the sensate and extra-physical realms. We paid attention to premonitions, heart stirrings and communications from beyond the grave. We heeded omens and followed lunar and solar cycles and the calendar of seasons. Today, in a world of intense mental activity, we have lost the ability to listen to our heart. Amidst the worries, preoccupations and stresses of daily living, the wisdom of the heart and the truth that is there have been silenced.

You need to open your heart once again so the Creator's Love can be born in your heart. This happens when you shun all else but the purity of God's Love, the beauty of the divine presence, the glory of divine Light. As you open your heart, you find silence, a silence that is at the core of the soul's existence. Only in this silence can God's presence be felt, for how can one be conscious of such tender and divine Love in the din of distraction, the noise of the senses, the commotion of emotions? It is in the peace, stillness and silence of your heart that God's Love can settle and abide within you. You prepare for this through the silence of meditation and prayer and by inviting stillness into your life.

Silence is found in the core of your being where complete peace abides in the stillness of Love, the quietude of the Light. There is a sacred space in your heart where you are alive, alert, in absolute awareness of the divine presence. In this silence, peace and awareness the Creator enters. Nothing else can enter this core of your being. Nothing else can touch it, but the Creator. If your Beloved is not there, it is empty and you feel this emptiness as a great loss or an immense longing. Yet when the heart is free of sensory influences, when it is unencumbered by the domination of the ego, it is pure. In its purity, the heart is the perfect place for the Creator to dwell within you.

It is in the sacred space of your heart where God creates his divine child, where you transcend separation and become One with the Creator. Your blessed unity with God is your birthright and through it you join the eternal flow of infinite being. You are born again. And what does this rebirth mean? It is the coming forth of consciousness of your spiritual self. You are aware that you are not your physical self; you are spirit and your spirit is one with the Creator. You are reborn into the true Reality of spirit and you begin a new life in the planes of Light. You are reborn into the Light.

Being who you are, a divine child, there is nothing you cannot do. I have come to give you this message. I have come to remind you about Love and I have come to do this as a manifestation of the Creator's Love for you. It is you who will rise up and radiate Light to the world. You are the Light of the world and the world needs your Light now.

In the stage of transcendence, you acknowledge the oneness that you are with the Creator and because of this oneness you understand that there is no absence of anything. The Creator is everything, contains everything within his self, infinitely. So nothing is missing, ever. If you are one with the Creator, and the Creator is everything, how can there be a lack of anything? What more can you possibly need or want? There is nothing else to need, nothing else to want. If God is All, then there can be nothing that is not God.

The only yearning that exists at this level of your spiritual evolution is yearning for the Creator. All other yearning, all other desire is false and derives from the illusory reality of the ego. "I want a BMW." "If I had a romantic partner I'd be fulfilled." "If my daughter were accepted in University, I would be happy." The romance, the car, the daughter will not satisfy the fundamental yearning of your heart. Yearning to be whole, yearning for eternity, yearning to be Home with the Creator, this is the true craving of the heart.

The Love of the Creator sustains you like the air you bring into your lungs every moment. You may feel a longing in your heart for the tender radiance of divine Love. You might enter into a very deep darkness to awaken to the true nature of this longing. As in all spiritual matters, the solution to this ache, this longing in your heart is so simple.

First, open your heart to the Creator's Love. It is there, always available to you for it IS you.

Second, connect to the presence of the Creator that is the energy you feel in your body and all around you. The divine Presence and Love are what you are made of. Once this presence is felt in every cell in your body, it will always be there. You will be firmly planted in the moment and deeply attuned to who you really are.

Opening your heart and feeling the Creator's presence in your being is the beginning of a beautiful journey of discovery and realization that you are not a separate being. You are One with the Love and with All-That-Is. The realization of this Love will fill all emptiness with radiant Light.

And your thoughts cease. You may have been told, as I was, to stay in the moment, to let everything go, to stop your mind so you can reach a state of thoughtless presence. During years of meditation practice when I attempted to control my thoughts, it had been impossible for me to use the mind to control my thinking. This attempt to control only made my mind stronger and thoughts more persistent. It was such a relief to discover that I had been doing it backwards and that the way to a mind devoid of useless thought was simple. In a flash of inspiration that was as beautiful as it was profound, the Creator showed me the true way to calm thoughts and quiet the mind: through Him. The advice I had received from many sources on calming the mind invariably omitted the essential element in attaining enlightenment: the Creator.

Once you open your heart, consciously aware of your soul, loving the Creator and feeling his Presence in your being; your thoughts cease automatically. Your mind is silent and you are immersed in the deep pool of the present moment. Rather than trying to force the mind to be silent and in the moment, and from there reach the deep recesses of your heart where the Creator's Presence dwells; you begin by being conscious of the Creator's Presence, feeling the Love and feeling the magnificent Light. The mind surrenders its hold completely and you are pulled into the present moment.

Union with the Creator is, after all, the purpose of our life's journey and it is the goal of our spiritual practice. The aim of a spiritual practice is not to be in the moment or quiet the mind as recommended in many spiritual disciplines. Though controlling your thoughts and staying in the moment may be a means to enlightenment, these practices may not be the most beneficial place to start. When you are in your heart, aware of the Creator's presence within you; you are in the moment, all thoughts stop and the ego weakens its hold. It is much easier and effective to begin your spiritual journey by fostering God-consciousness. Once awareness of the Creator is attained, everything else falls into place. Not the other way around. Be conscious of the Creator's presence at all times, with an open heart, and you will awaken to the reality of who you are: One with the Creator. At that instant, you are in the moment, unperturbed by useless thoughts and you are aware of who you truly are.

Of course, all thoughts do not cease. Thoughts are necessary and God-given and we need our faculties to function so we may do God's work. As we think, speak and perform our daily activities, we are still aware of the Creator's presence in us and around us. Thought may co-exist peacefully with God-consciousness. However, when you are meditating, engaged in prayer or in contemplation it is useful for thought to take a back seat and allow the presence of the Creator to come through in all Its magnificence. This cessation of thought may be brief, but it will have a powerful impact on your heart, your soul and your connection with the Creator.

Our souls embarked on a long and arduous journey when we separated from the Creator. Our separation was entirely voluntary. God never pushed us out; it was we who wanted to experience otherness. Our experience of separation began in higher dimensions and as we hurled downwards, our souls suffered damage. This damage is called the ego. The ego trapped us in form, tied us to time and space, made complexity our rule, and we closed our hearts in fear of the Creator, convinced by our egos that the Creator would punish us for leaving our home. We closed our hearts to the Love eternal and we gripped the gnarled roots of the ego that would not allow us to let go and surrender. An essential element in returning to the Creator is surrendering completely. This is impossible when our hearts are closed by fear.

When a part of our consciousness decided to separate from our Source, our souls, the multiple dimensions and the physical world were created so that we might have the experiences that we desired. Our soul remains connected in part with our spirit, which is the uncreated part of us that is in union with God. The soul is an intermediate aspect of ourselves that connects us on one side to the world we live in physically and, on the other side, to our spirit that is connected to the Creator. The spiritual heart is in the core of our soul and holds within itself a deep-seated yearning to return to complete union with God. It is our soul that carries the inextinguishable impulse to return to the Creator, to be One with All-That-Is.

To return to your Source you increase the Light that you hold, that is, the spiritual vibrations of God's Love, so you can return to your true self as spirit. As mentioned before, between God's Light and the soul, there is spirit.

Spirit is what keeps your soul connected to God's Light, to its divine nature, while it can touch the world of matter. The spirit is that part of you that is uncreated. It is the divine part of your being that is eternally and infinitely connected to the Creator. It has always been and always will be. It is the Creator's spark. When you become One with the Creator, your soul dissolves in the Light and you become pure spirit.

Your soul is the impulse that moves you toward the Creator and assists you in returning Home to your Source. Your soul is a crucial ally in your journey to union with the Creator. In most persons, the soul is ignored and the senses become dominant. When this happens, most of the soul remains in the spiritual planes enjoying the Light. However, when someone awakens to the reality of the Light, the soul takes over its role as spiritual guide and begins to prepare the person for the journey ahead. The soul knows what it needs to do to return to the Creator's embrace. Once a person is unhindered by the ego's dominance, it can listen to the soul's guidance and by doing so learn all he or she needs to know to unite with God. Your soul's mission is to show you the way back to the Creator, to guide you Home.

In this task, the soul lifts you spiritually as the soul can easily ascend to the highest planes of Light where it connects to spirit and reaches the Creator's realm of Light. The soul has only one desire and that is to be turned to the Creator at all times, loving the Creator always. The soul is filled with longing to be one with God. Your soul is in constant movement toward God. When you live within the sacred space of your heart, within this light of the soul, you live in the heart of the Creator. Here you are one with the Creator in a true unity that no one can divide. The One manifests in many ways, but it is only One. You are a spark of Light, a part of the One.

As the part of the Creator that is pure spirit, we share many of the Creator's attributes. The Creator is eternal and we are eternal, the Creator is unconditional Love and we are unconditional Love, the Creator is only One, and we are One with the Creator. The Creator is an omnipresent Light and as pure spirit, we bask in the Light of the Creator and delight in the Creator's Love.

As you enter into the chamber of transcendence in your journey to union with God, you are aware of your divine nature and are conscious of the presence of God within you most of the time. You are aware that the separation you felt previously from the Creator is only an apparent separation. It was an illusion created by your ego to keep you stranded in the desert island of its own domination. The Creator never rejects us. We are the ones who turn our backs on the Creator when we allow the distractions of the world to open a chasm of separation between our selves and our Source.

In the stage of transcendence, you understand fully that your soul is the mediating consciousness between your spirit and your physical body and you make the conscious effort to live your life as soul, turning always toward spirit, toward the Creator. You know that your spirit is your True Self that has never separated from the Creator.

In this stage, you continue to purify your heart through prayer and meditation, through good deeds and awareness of God. The purer your heart, the more powerful and stronger your connection with the Creator.

A pure heart can accomplish miracles. A pure heart is completely surrendered to the Creator, wanting nothing, desiring nothing, but to be in Oneness with divine Love. A pure heart has no worries, commitments or burdens. And this is what you pray for, to purify your heart to such an extent that you desire nothing but complete union with the Creator.

Your ego is calmer in the stage of transcendence, but still active since the ego has no sense of rest. It is forever striving, always rushing forward to attain something beyond its grasp. Peace is not possible in the domain of the ego. If you seek peace in the strivings of the ego, it will not be there. If you seek peace in other persons, places or situations that are the domain of the ego, you will never find it. Buddha advised us to look for peace within and not depend on it in any other place. "There are no waves in the depths of the ocean," he said, "it is still and unbroken."

It is important to take every opportunity to continue working on the dissolution of your ego, so you may experience peace in your heart. To find peace, first surrender all desire, including the desire for peace, and go deep within the sacred space of your heart. That is your connection to God. That is where you dwell in the sweetness of the Creator's Love.

The more you give up your ego, the more you remove your personality self from what you do, the easier it is to be conscious of God within yourself. Turn your heart towards the Creator in everything you do, in every thought you have. As you think about the Creator and allow the Creator to act through you, the Creator will always be with you no matter where you are or what the circumstances of your life may be. Keep the Creator in your thoughts, in your feelings at all times, wherever you are, whomever you are with. You will never be alone, for the Creator is with you always.

On many occasions, as a result of prayer or a particularly deep meditation, you may enter into the realm of bliss and even ecstasy. You feel such a profound all-encompassing love in your heart that tears spill from your eyes and you may even sustain an altered state of consciousness. Your being elevates and you feel as if you were walking on air. These rapturous moments are indeed beautiful. However, if you are always seeking them, you have fallen into the desire-bound domination of your ego. When you truly experience love and devotion to the Creator, there is no ecstasy, no bliss. You remain in the calm waters of a clear pond unruffled, unmoved, in a state of being Love. As you are Love, you are Love every moment, and this Love does not move you into states that when they are gone remind you of something lost or emptied.

Love is much higher than the sensation of rapture. Love pierces your heart and remains there in the sacred space as a gentle caress, never to dissolve or disappear or lose its potency. It is there, in full force, when you are of service to others in the name of the Creator, when you are an instrument of God's Love. If you are in the middle of a meditation, enjoying fully the ecstasy of the Creator's presence and someone knocks at your door asking for help, it is best to give up the ecstasy of the moment and help the person who needs you. At that moment, you surrender truly to God's will and blessings will come to you multiplied.

Continue to surrender all to the Creator, including your will, your very life, all life and in the end you surrender even love. Your will merges with the Creator's will and then you are completely content with what the Creator does.

Don't be concerned with the mistakes you have made, the errors you have committed. No matter how grievous your actions, once you surrender to the Creator with purity of heart, the past is erased by a big swoop of Grace. Remember that God is. God is always in the present because the present is all that is. The moment of surrender to the Creator is in the present and there is no past only the purity of your heart at that moment. The Creator embraces you at that instant of surrender and the embrace is eternal and infinite. The past dissolves in the magnificent vastness of the Creator's Love.

Love the Creator completely and you will love others so much better when you love them through the filter of the Creator's Love. When you love through the Creator, you are united to all living beings, you are united to the world and all of existence becomes one. As you enjoy this unity, transcending your body, your emotions, your desires you realize that the Creator's Love illuminates everything you do. Everything you touch is touched by Love.

Once you have awakened to a new reality and purify your heart, you enter into a state of blissful transcendence and you begin to free your mind from the ego's grasp. You do this by being aware of the Creator at all times, under all circumstances. You acquire God-consciousness by letting go of all unnecessary thoughts. As thoughts arise, you let them go without dwelling on them. You don't allow the mind to latch on to thoughts and become lost in the chaos of disorganized thinking. Once the mind is free, it can sustain spiritualized thoughts and be in harmony with the Mind of God. As the mind is no longer distracted by unnecessary thoughts, it turns to God and you transcend the mind itself and find the divinity within you.

When you reach transcendence, you live the peace of God-consciousness.

The less you are aware of God, the less peace you have. So you can determine your level of God-consciousness by the peace you feel or your lack of peace. For God is peace.

God-consciousness is a necessary aspect of transcendence. You are aware that the Creator is already in you, closer than your breath. It is so easy. Just enter into your heart with the full awareness that the Creator is there. As you are conscious of God, you love him because he is. You love God for the pure sake of loving him. You love the Creator in every action, every thought you have, every word you speak. And the more you do this, the more you love him. You forget yourself in the Love.

In transcendence you relinquish the hold of the past and the future and abide in the present moment. The easiest and fastest way to be in the present moment is by being conscious of the Divine Presence within your heart. Consciousness of the Creator's presence brings you into the present moment, an eternal flow with no beginning, no end, with no past, no future. All that exists is an eternal flow that stretches out into infinity. As you float in this eternal flow of the moment, there is nothing else but the moment. There, at that point of stillness and absolute peace, the Creator waits for you. He has always been there, you just weren't conscious of it. The Creator never leaves. He is there, every instant. All you have to do is be aware, acknowledge, be conscious of the Creator's presence in your heart.

When I entered this stage, the nature of my prayers changed. I realized that there is no need to pray to ask for anything. The only prayer, which is an ongoing communication with the Creator, is to become more and more One with his Love, to love him more. During transcendence, you are aware of the Creator's presence in your heart every instant of your life: during work, conversations with others as well as during meditation, prayer and contemplation.

You never let God-awareness be detached from your consciousness and you are rewarded with the blessing of Grace in your heart. You transcend the physical and absorbed in the Creator's Love, your physical self becomes an instrument of the Creator's Will and your spiritual self steps up to reclaim your identity as a divine child, God's child. Your prayer becomes a constant connection with the Beloved.

In this stage you realize that praying for something is useless so you pray for desirelessness. When you desire nothing only that you may love God, then everything is given to you. Everything has already been given to you anyway. You just need to realize it.

Be aware of how you pray and why. Often instead of praying we attempt to make deals with the Creator. This is what we do when we perform good deeds, pray and behave in certain ways so that the Creator will give us something in return or do something that we want to have done. When we are sick, we pray to the Creator for health and in doing so we admit that our health is more important than the Creator. To free yourself from praying to the Creator for something, trying to make deals with the Creator or otherwise interacting with the Creator for personal gain; surrender to the Creator completely and be his instrument in everything you do. When you surrender your will to the Creator, then the Creator's Will is done in you.

Prayer, as it is conventionally done, is ineffective. The Creator already knows what you want and need. True prayer is ceaseless gratitude to God for everything that is. True prayer is acting in a loving way, being kind to others solely for your love of God. St Augustine said: "You pray to what you love, for true, whole prayer is nothing but love!" So we pray by loving the Creator in all things, all the time and being grateful for the Creator's blessings. This is prayer without ceasing.

In the stage of transcendence Grace comes to you as you recognize that you were born as a divine child and that God is present within you every instant. Grace then flows to you with a new Light and this Light is a divine essence that pours into your heart. The Light in your heart grows and becomes so luminous it sparkles in countless particles and radiates through your body. It infuses your aura and continues radiating outwards into your surroundings. Your heart, your soul, the core of your being overflow with this Light, which is the perfect manifestation of God's Love. It touches everything within you and around you.

When your heart turns to the Creator, in that very instant of awareness of the Creator, the Light begins to sparkle and glow. It awakens your heart, calls your soul to you, and you begin a process of rapid transformation where you transcend your physical body and reside in the Light. Your soul takes over and you are guided into higher and higher realms. Your speech changes, your actions change, your emotions are subdued and your ego continues the arduous process of dissolving which began during the purification process. You begin to act and think in a kind and loving way in every situation of your life. You begin to reside in the joy of your spiritual self that is always connected to the Creator. As you are imbued by divine Love, awakened to divine Light, you turn away from anything that threatens your joy, your inner peace, the tender stillness of your being. You protect the Light within you.

The more you live within the Creator's Light, the more discernment you show in your choices. You no longer wish to spend time in relationships or pursuits that keep you from the Light. You are freer to be who you really are: the Creator's beloved child, the Creator's spark. And you shun the enticements of the ego, its unnecessary thoughts, desires, attachments, emotions and delusions.

You see that this Light, this Grace, is not found outside of yourself. You have looked for it on the outside and not found it. It was only when you looked within your heart and opened your heart to the Creator that the Light came through with all its magnificence and filled you with a Love that has no name, for to name it Love is not enough.

And when you experience the radiance of this Love, the beauty of this Light, you understand how scattered your senses had made you feel in the past. How your ego had convinced you that you knew nothing and sent you off in an endless search that distracted you from discovering the treasure within your heart. Now you see that there is wisdom, a knowledge within you that has been unlocked, revealed by the Light. And you marvel at how much you know, how much you understand and realize.

All you have to do to find the Creator, to hear his Word in your heart, to attain God-consciousness is to plunge into the stillness of your heart. In the silence, you will find him. Silence is found behind every sound, behind every emotion and behind every thought. Silence shines like a bright spark in the night and calls to you the splendor of the Creator's Love.

Silence is the stillness and peace you find once the clamor of the ego has been eradicated and you desire nothing but to fill yourself with the Creator's essence. In silence you hear the Creator's word and your heart is transformed. In silence, your heart opens. In silence, you can look into the Creator's heart and feel the vastness of his Love. In silence, you are lost in the vastness and become One with the Creator.

You are made perfect, not by anything you do, or say, or think. You are made perfect by the Love in your heart.

You need to forget yourself, forget others, forget the world, forget your senses, forget all that you know, all that you have learned. Forget your feelings, forget your knowledge. None of this will help you reach God-consciousness, for the Creator is in the purity of silence. It is in silence, when you are doing nothing, making no effort, just being, that the Creator slips quietly into your heart. He has always been there, but the awareness of his presence occurs in the silence, in the stillness of your heart.

To reach transcendence it is important not to turn away from the Creator. You turn away from the Creator with distractions, by dwelling in the past or anticipating the future, by allowing your emotions to control you. You turn away from the Creator when you lack forgiveness, when you judge, when you hurt yourself or others. You turn away from the Creator when you do not love. You turn away from the Creator definitively when you close your heart.

Be aware of the ego, which has not yet dissolved at this stage. It may try to convince you that you are spiritually evolved and may even persuade you that you are spiritually superior to others. You may find yourself judging those who are not at the level you think you are. You might even be critical of others' imperfections, not understanding that what you criticize may not be imperfections but differences in the way they are walking their path. Be aware of the arrogance that may set in as others contact you for guidance, as you are recognized as someone who is "spiritual." You might even begin to feel proud of the good deeds that you do and believe that it is you who brings healing and Light into the hearts of others forgetting that you are an instrument of the Creator's Love. Be ever alert of the ego's wiles at this stage especially.

Be honest with yourself regarding your spiritual progress and identify the areas you need to strengthen. Be especially aware of your love for others. Is it heartfelt and unconditional? Or have you convinced yourself mentally that you love someone, but feel nothing for this person in your heart? Observe how effectively you are performing your spiritual work as an instrument, rather than as a personal or even prideful act. You will receive many warnings from your soul if you are not advancing or happen to fall back. The alerts will be abundant and consist of lack of peace, incessant or obsessive thoughts, uncontrollable emotions, judgment of others. You may begin to find pleasure in the company of people and in activities that are not conducive to spiritual growth. You may also receive messages in your dreams. Every effort should be made to stay on track, intent on reaching the apex of the pyramid, embracing the Beloved.

At this stage of your journey, it is essential that you protect your light. Beware of the pitfalls that may cause you to backslide. If necessary, return to the chamber of purification to regain the purity of your heart. If every time you talk to certain persons you feel depressed or badly, these persons are detracting from your light and you should avoid them. If there is an activity you engage in that takes you out of your heart, then there is no Light in this activity and you should not engage in it. If there are certain thoughts that make you feel angry, guilty, sad, anxious or doubting, then these are not Light-filled thoughts and you should attempt to choose thoughts that bring Light to your life rather than gloom.

Protect your light. Remember always to be conscious that you are a spark of the Creator and turn your heart toward the Light at all times.

It is possible that at this stage of your journey you may grapple, as I did for a long time, with the concept of evil. Even though you are enjoying your stay at the luminous chamber of transcendence, you inevitably notice that the world is pervaded by what seems like a limitless onslaught of problems that locks humanity into a state of fear, anxiety and physical illness. It may seem that most people experience a sense of separateness that creates feelings of not belonging and may lead to emotional and physical problems and even to war and other acts of violence. In this world of havoc, you may ask yourself whether there is a reason, or even a purpose for the negativity in the world, for the many instances of evil.

In many internal conversations between my soul and the Creator I was made aware that evil is the complete lovelessness that results from ego-domination. Those who practice evil are in the most terrible pain as they have relinquished the Creator's Love in favor of the power of the ego. Ego is suffering because it is the absence of God. Ego is the anti-soul. The ego erects an image of negativity, of evil, of suffering and fear in its attempt to impose a sense of separation. It creates a veil within us that does not allow us to see the Truth.

Negative energy is not real. It is the ego that makes it seem real. Negativity is a product of the ego's delusions and it has no power. The only power is the Creator. Nothing negative can exist in the Creator's Reality, which is the true Reality. Once we recognize that this is so, all negativity dissolves. It just fades away. At that moment of recognition, we open ourselves to the Creator's Presence, to the Creator's abundance, to all Good. And there is no more poverty, fear or negativity in our hearts. Negativity is the result of not knowing ourselves, not dwelling in the true Reality of the Creator's Light.

Negative energy is fueled by our negative thoughts and intent, negative emotions, drama, negative acts, in other words, by the instruments of the ego. As the density of the energy becomes entrenched, it forms entities that are non-feeling. Devoid of emotions, negative entities react rather than act. They are like a virus that needs to feed from a host in order to stay alive. Every time we have a negative thought or emotion; every time we utter negative words; whenever we fall into the clutches of drama; when we do something that is not ethical and harm or hurt another living being, we feed the negative forces. This darkness, created by us, can become a pandemic as in instances of war and massacres, and spread harmful contaminants everywhere. It is possible to eradicate the contagion with a special vaccine: the serum of Love. In the Light of the Creator's Love negativity cannot exist.

In this stage of your spiritual evolution, you reach a deep understanding that the only reality is the Creator and since the Creator and we are One, negativity cannot dwell within us unless we invite it in by giving it a reality it does not have. As we acknowledge that nothing exists outside of the Creator, all the false powers of negativity dissolve. Every time you are conscious of the Creator's presence, every time you are aware of your oneness with God, the frequency of your vibration lifts and everyone around you is lifted also, beyond negativity and into the Light.

In the stage of transcendence rapture may be experienced, sometimes frequently. Rapture is an experience common to mystics[5] whereby the person is transported into a higher state of being during meditation, contemplation[6], prayer or while in communion with nature. The person experiences a spiritual exaltation, a sudden opening of the heart, a shift in consciousness in which he or she is acutely aware of God's presence. The experience can be described as one of ecstasy and brings with it an expansion of awareness and, in many, tears of bliss.

During states of rapture many things are revealed to you and you have no doubt that the revelations are true. There is direct communication between your soul and God. In an instant, knowledge is imparted and suddenly you know many things of a spiritual nature that you had not known before. Revelations are frequently communicated without words.

There are several clear signs to indicate transcendence or God-consciousness. First, you see the Creator in everything and everyone (including yourself). When you look at a person, or a tree, or a bee, your heart opens and you say or think or feel: *there too is the Creator.*

---

5   Mystics are those who have an impassioned desire for union with God and dedicate their lives to its attainment. They have a strong conviction that God is All and we are part of that All. Mysticism is a path of the heart that seeks to transcend the limitations of the ego, surrender to God and dwell in blissful union with our Creator.

6   Contemplation is a state of awareness of God's being through an act of devotion, through a focus on spiritual things.

Second, for transcendence to exist, there must be a true surrender of everything. You let go of attachments, desires, wishes of attainment. You know that the Creator is in you, nurturing your heart, your soul, so there is nothing that you want, nothing that you desire. You do not even desire a blessing, or need it, for you know it is there, alive, incandescent in your heart. So you let go of everything, attach to nothing and be as an empty vessel.

Third, you love everything and everyone, including yourself unconditionally. Love is the sweetest link that connects you to the Creator. Whatever you do, no matter how trivial or simple, if done with love in your heart, it brings you closer to the Creator than any epic deeds done without love. To live as pure essence, as the divine child that you truly are, you must love the Creator in all persons and things, love all others as you love your closest friends and family. As long as you are more concerned with yourself and the people close to you than you are with strangers, then you have not acquired transcendence. If you don't love yourself, loving others is impossible. You love others as one person and you love the Creator in them.

Fourth, you look at the world through the prism of gratitude. You are grateful for everything and everyone, even the difficult lessons in life, even losses. Gratitude is the most potent engine that powers true Love. The more grateful you are, the more your heart will open to unconditional Love.

Fifth, you stop searching. You are still and quiet and content in the knowingness that the Creator is in you, that you are part of the Creator and that everything and everyone is in and you are in everything and everyone. You act from your heart, from your soul and you never ask "why?"

For everything you do is done with the Creator in your intentions, in your heart. Not because you want the Creator's blessing, or because you want to attain the Creator's approval. But because you want nothing and as you want nothing from the Creator, you simply love him and through this love you act, you speak, you think, you breathe. There is nothing else, but your love. You empty yourself of all knowledge and seek only to enter the sacred space of your heart. There is nothing to seek outside of your heart.

Sixth, you let go of all ideas you have of the Creator, for you know that the mind will never know the Creator and that the more complex your idea of the Creator, the more this idea will keep the Creator away from you. As you let go of the idea of the Creator, he will slip in through the silence of your heart. God created us through Love. Love is God and this Love contains the whole world, all of existence. We are all on our way to our highest perfection in Love. The truth of this Love breaks open our hearts into the eternity that is there.

Finally, you are deeply aware that when there is love, gratitude and desirelessness in your heart, the Creator is there always with you, infinitely present, closer to you than your breath. At this stage you feel great love for everyone and see God in everyone. You are conscious of God's presence in you and in everyone and everything around you. You no longer care for earthly things except those that you can use to be of service to God and to humanity.

The most important realization in the stage of transcendence, which brings the deepest joy and fulfillment, is to know that the Creator is Love and from this Love he gives life to all in existence. Nothing exists separate from the Creator's Love.

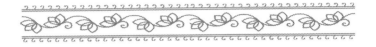

Surrender

You are so close now to the apex of the pyramid. You enter this fourth chamber, the stage of surrender, with determination. You are strengthened by a spiritual will that propels you upwards, higher and higher on the spiral staircase to God. You transcend completely all vestiges of desire, all thoughts, all emotions. In the emptiness that remains, you are alone with the Beloved. You are not concerned with the how and the why and the where. You simply rest in divine Love and devote your life to the Creator. You relish opportunities to be alone. You renounce whatever disturbs your solitary enjoyment of peace. The Creator's Love is your only comfort.

And what is the Creator's Love? It is the secret revealed to all souls who remain in silence waiting for its appearance. Divine Love is the consciousness of the Creator, the awareness of the Creator. It is the knowingness of the Creator's presence in you. Love is being aware of a Light in your heart that like a sparkling sun brings a perfect peace into your being. It is an eternal, infinite and vast Light. Your heart opens to its sublime resonance.

Before attaining union with the Creator, your heart must burst open in an act of total surrender. You empty yourself out of everything else, surrender to the Creator completely – without any doubts or concerns, in complete trust– and in an instant the gift of Grace comes through. You surrender and you know without any doubt that you are transformed.

Everything changes.

But you must choose whether you wish to surrender and experience this transformation. The choice is always up to you.

Choices present themselves bright as glass. A path cleaves in two or three or five, like an open hand. Before us are the tantalizing prospects of different directions, calling us with the mystery each holds, pointing at a multitude of possibilities. We stand at the crossroad, heart hammering in our chest, and we ponder the best route to take, the one that will lead to that ephemeral dream of happiness.

Whichever path we choose, the decision is our own, a confirmation of our will to select one among many possibilities. Our choice is our possession. We guard it closely with sincere conviction and commitment because this choice will be with us forever, coloring all our acts not only with its own separate possibilities, but reminding us always of the other paths we did not walk. We choose our way and we live with our choice.

There is a point, a moment we arrive at where the inevitable strikes us with its adamant presence. If we have not chosen a path of Light, we plunge into a space of sadness, futile longing and confusion. But when we choose the Light, this choice brings us inside our soul where we recognize the Creator, the Father of Lights[7], in our heart.

The chamber of surrender is beautiful beyond words. Here you gaze at the luminous facets of the quartz pyramid and become lost in its patterns of Light, in the infinity that is reflected in its mirrors. As you turn your back completely to the world of illusion of the ego, the world of the senses, your awareness is heightened. You see, with absolute clarity, the reality of your being. And you hear a tone, a vibration, a song of love. As the song soars to the highest planes, it simultaneously burrows inside your soul. And your entire being dissolves into the harmony of the song. You are infused with an infinite peace, the deepest Love. You surrender to the Love.

As you surrender deeper and deeper to the Love, you transmute all the impermanent experiencing of the ego into radiant Light. You transcend the false ego-reality. This is what Jesus meant when he said, at the moment of his crucifixion: "I have overcome the world."

When you surrender, visionary encounters with God may occur frequently. One evening the sun was dropping in the west and its yellow rays glittered through the branches and leaves of the trees outside my window. A beam of sunlight pierced my eyes and I became one with the Light. In an instant I recognized that the Creator is my Light. That night I was awakened by a tap in my heart. The Creator spoke to me through my soul. He communicated that I had finally understood the Light. That until that day I had believed that the Light came to me from the outside, from Source, but that I finally

---

7   St. James often referred to God as the Father of Lights.

understood that I am his spark and I am Light. Then, in a moment of sparkling clarity I understood that everyone is God's Light. It is the ego that mars our souls to such an extent that the soul, which is a spark of the Creator, is unable to express itself in its truth. When I understood that, I truly understood God, the Creator, the beginning and end, the Absolute. The Creator revealed to me that I could see Reality with perfect clarity. Wisdom is mine because the soul already knows everything and what we call learning lessons is really remembering what we already know. All knowledge, all wisdom, all Love is already within me. God is Perfect Love and so am I. At that moment I was graced with insight, with clear sight. I was illumined with full awareness, living the now.

Then the Creator revealed that I needed to go out into the world with the message that we are all God. Every being, every thing is God. There is nothing but God. The path of Light that awakens us to this realization arises from the silence of the heart.

Within the heart, in the deepest core of your being, is a sacred space where the Creator dwells. The divine presence is there in a point of Light that when entered into, spirals inward into an infinite space of Light. This is the seat of all Love, this is the seat of all Light. It is the Throne of God. And it is contained inside each living being. As this point of Light in the sacred space of the heart spirals outward, it expands like a pulsating galaxy and gathers everything within itself, within the Light.

Your heart opens in oscillating waves radiating farther and farther out and you realize that you are in the heart of the Creator, in the breath of the Creator. You see that

All is the Creator and you are All in the Creator. The Creator is in you and you are in the Creator and as your consciousness expands inward and reaches outward, there is no difference. The inner planes of Light are one with the outer planes and you become aware of the sacred dance of existence, round and round, without end.

And you marvel at the beauty of it.

Your heart, this spiritual organ of Love, reflects this Truth for you, like a calm lake. Becoming, always becoming.

Dominated as we are by our senses, we spend our precious time on Earth asking questions or trying to understand Absolute Reality versus illusion or whether life is finite or infinite. We spend countless hours on the Internet or with our noses stuck in books, feeding our ego's insatiable hunger for facts. In the meantime, we have not been doing our spiritual practice, which is the only thing that will bring us to union with our Beloved.

Yet, if you surrender to the Creator, truly surrender, not in your mind but from your heart, surrendering everything including your life, there will be nothing else in your life except the Creator and this devotion to our Beloved will guide you through life and bring you to a blessed union.

Whether all is an illusion or not, whether we are infinite or not, whether problems exist or not, whether there are beings in other universes or not, nothing else matters at that moment of surrender. The moment of surrender becomes every moment. We surrender and in an instant we see the Light of God. We realize who we are and why we are here. At that moment, we make the commitment, because we know that this is what we were meant to do, to help others discover the Light in their hearts.

Finding the Creator within the sacred space of your heart and surrendering completely to him brings you instantly into a spiritualized state of great wisdom, dwelling fully in the Creator's Light. To accomplish this goal, you must empty yourself of everything through purification until you reach a state of desirelessness where you want nothing, desire nothing. As you are stripped of everything, the Creator will come and fill you like a rich wine fills an empty glass.

At that moment, when you are so empty that the Creator can slip into your heart gently and tenderly, you experience the instant of surrender. You surrender all to the Creator and as you surrender, you are completely an instrument of the Creator's will. The Creator directs you, chooses for you, speaks through you. You die to the world so you may live for the Beloved.

Purification is the blessed preparation you do for Grace to flood into your heart so you may transcend your senses, your physical being and reach out to the Beloved. You purify yourself through prayer, meditation, by being mindful of your thoughts and actions. You purify your heart by doing good, healing yourself and forgiving. Then, as you transcend your ego, in a moment of sparkling beauty, you surrender yourself completely to the Creator. You say to the Creator: "I surrender everything to you. I only desire what You, in Your Divine Wisdom will give me. And even that, I surrender."

Thus you begin a phase of spiritual evolution that is essential for union. You continue surrendering every single thing that you are, that you own, that you have, that you desire, that you wish for. You surrender all of your attachments, the veil that does not allow you to see Reality and everything that keeps you from union with God.

You realize that there is nothing else but the Beloved, so you allow yourself to live for his Love, to live for his Light that fills your heart with sweetness and peace. You dissolve in the Love. You give yourself entirely to the Love. You love others in God.

Then you ask the Creator to fill you with more Light so that you can continue dissolving your ego, removing the veil that still blinds you to the Truth, dissolving all the obstacles that do not allow you to see the true Reality that you are one with All-That-Is. You notice that the purity of the Creator's Light cleanses everything. You let the Light push everything that is not Love away from you. You do this with the stillness of peace in your heart.

You feel the Love of the Creator deep in your heart. It is a Light that shimmers and glows, so radiant and beautiful; in your body, your heart, your soul, all around you. You feel the Light glowing in your heart, in all the cells in your body until every part of you is Light. You let the Light flow and as you surrender more and more the Light removes all obstacles, all blockages, all negativity. Everything in you is only Light, only Love. You feel how all unbalanced energy washes out of you and you glow with the Light as you are willing to let go of everything else, so only the Love of the Creator can dwell in your heart. And this too, you surrender until you are left with nothing.

Trust is the necessary requisite of surrender. Trust is what empowers Love, propels your devotion. It is the backbone of your service to the Creator. Without trust, your heart cannot open to the Creator's Love. Trust in the Creator is essential for union. When you pray that the Creator's will be done, then when it is not what you expect, don't be disappointed. Trust and accept with joy the Creator's will. Say to the Creator: "Give me the confidence to want what You will." This is trust. When you trust completely in the Creator, then you love the Creator with the perfection of a pure heart.

The Creator will never fail you. The Creator will manifest wonderful things through you when you place your trust in him. When you don't trust, your love diminishes and a crack opens in your heart through which fear can enter. Once fear has entered into your heart, it blocks your God-consciousness and brings to you doubt, confusion and other emotions that drive you away from the Creator and the splendor of divine Love. Only Love can dispel the fear, uncertainty and mistrust. When you turn your heart to the Creator with trust, certainty and love and all you do and think of and wish for is filled with the Creator, then everything will manifest the way it should.

As long as you are full of worries, fears and distractions, thinking about superficialities, mired in complexity you are empty of the Creator and surrender is impossible. You are full of the Creator when you are empty of everything else. You cannot be conscious of the Creator's presence when your heart is cluttered with debris. The Creator comes to the purity of silence, the purity of clarity, the purity of emptiness.

To fully surrender, then, you must empty yourself out of everything else and be still in the unwavering trust that God's presence will fill you completely. Once you do this, you do not need anything else. You do not strive or seek, for everything has been given to you. God is everything. You rest in this contentment and you surrender to the Creator all that you are. You renew your surrender daily in everything you do.

When you truly surrender to the Beloved Creator, you live for his Love that fills your heart with sweetness and peace. As you surrender to the immensity of the Creator's Love, you allow the Love to be the only thing present in you. You surrender everything you think is important. You surrender your attachments, your desires, your ceaseless thoughts, your drama. You surrender who and what you think you are. You surrender your ego. You surrender your whole self to the Creator and feel the peace, the joy, the beauty of this surrender. You give it all up in an instant and say to the Creator: "My Beloved, I surrender all of this to You. I surrender everything that keeps me from being One with Your Love." Then, you let everything go. You release everything that is not Love. As you surrender everything, your whole being fills with Light.

As you reach this state of desirelessness, of emptiness, when only the Creator dwells in your heart, there is no need to pray for you know that everything has been given to you. You are in God's Kingdom. You feel the completeness of your being. There is only peace and rest.

You don't want to go anywhere, do anything, be anyone. You don't want to have anything. You let everything go. You release everything that is not Love. You keep on surrendering and allowing your heart to be pure. You enjoy deep stillness and peace. You accept the invitation to rest in the Creator's Sweet Embrace. As you surrender, you dissolve in the Creator's Love because you have arrived. Your search is over. You don't need to search for anything, or make any effort. You are Home, resting in the splendor of the Creator's magnificent Light.

The senses will not bring you to the Creator, the outer world will not bring you to the Creator, nor will your efforts. Although a path needs to be paved to prepare for the Creator's Grace; it is surrender, pure and simple that will allow this gift of Grace to pour forth. It is when you cease in your efforts, when all action, thoughts, desires are suspended and you float in the nothingness of being that the Creator gently touches your heart and transforms you forever.

It is a point of no return. You remain still, in the presence of pure consciousness, knowing nothing, wanting nothing, being nothing but awareness. With complete devotion and trust, you surrender your life, your being to God. You are no longer bound to family, to friends, to material belongings, to pleasures, desires or to the false reality of the senses. At that moment of surrender, you are propelled into a Light that is so pure, that only the Creator is capable of holding it in your heart. There you remain, suspended in a state of absolute Love. The Love flows into you and flows out of you. An eternal, infinite flow of God's Love that is everything.

If for any reason you should return from this state of surrender because you respond to the call of the world of the senses and fall back into the false reality of the ego –which can easily rebuild itself even after complete surrender— you plunge down the spiral staircase. Very quickly, you find yourself outside the gates of the pyramid as a result of your own choices.

We came to reside in the density of the world and we long to return to the pure state in which we were part of the divine wholeness of being. The density of the physical realm weighs us down. When we give up that density, when we turn from the world of the senses and transcend the ego, we are again light and free. We float easily upwards to the kingdom of the Beloved, to our Home.

Surrendering, giving up things and forgetting the self, is not an act of self-sacrifice. There are many people who sacrifice things in the name of God or religion or love. Yet they are very far from attainment of God-consciousness because they have not realized the Truth. When you truly surrender to the Creator and awaken to the truth of existence, you do so without any sense of self-sacrifice. You do it in Love because there is nothing else that you want or desire or seek. You do it because nothing else matters but your love for the Creator. This love is so great that it brings you into the nothingness of silence where you are in full awareness of the Creator's presence within you. The dust in your eyes is removed. The veil that blinds you dissolves. At that moment, the Creator begets his divine child in the sacred space of your heart. In a marvelous spiral of beauty and love, you are reborn in God. As you merge so perfectly with God, our Creator, there is nothing that can bring sorrow or gladness to your heart for your heart is full of the Creator and only the Creator can reside in you.

When you surrender, the Creator works through you from inside the sacred space of your heart and moves outward like a burst of radiance from the sun. When that happens, you find yourself radiating the Creator's Light to everyone who is open to receive it, to everyone who has asked for this gift of Grace.

To be able to surrender completely to the Creator, intend for the Light to enter the sacredness of who you are. Allow the Light to stream through you in all its magnificent spaciousness and luminosity. Then, from your heart, you surrender everything to God. The moment of surrender is a moment of ecstasy and bliss when the soul knows God's Love. This knowledge of God's Love is indescribable. It marks your soul forever.

Union

Since separating from the Creator, we are attempting to return. This return is an archetypal quest that is reflected in our myths, literature and religions. The quest for the Holy Grail that appears in many literary texts is an example of the archetypal quest to find God. The Holy Grail is a sacred vessel that can grant whoever finds it great spiritual powers. It is concealed in a mystical place and only those who are spiritually worthy have any possibility of finding it. In the same way, throughout our lives we seek the key that will open the door to the sacred for us.

In a famous Greek myth Jason sets out on a perilous journey to find a golden fleece that is hidden in a secret place, and when found, will allow him to reclaim his birthright. This reflects our own attempts to live our existence trying to reclaim our right to live as the children of God. When Odysseus sets out to return home to Ithaca, he also represents our own journey home, our struggle to return to our place in the Creator's Kingdom.

The many myths and stories that have evolved throughout our history in which a person sets off on a dangerous quest to find a treasure that will transform him, represent our journey to find the treasure that will make us whole, redeem our birthright as children of God, reignite the spark of the Creator inside us.

Union with the Creator is our Holy Grail, our golden fleece, our Ithaca. When we came to Earth we vowed to undertake an arduous journey that, though filled with risks, wrong turns and distractions, we are willing to travel in order to reclaim our birthright as children of God and return Home to the Creator's loving Embrace. Through an awakening of our consciousness to the Light, we hold a map that guides us through a process of awakening, purification, transcendence and surrender to finally find the truth of our existence and dwell in the realm of Light where we belong with our Father of Lights. The soul is purified when all complexity and multiplicity is purged from it so it may enter into union with God. This occurs when the fractured material world is brought together in oneness and the soul rises to the planes where duality does not exist.

Union is when the soul surrenders completely and enters consciously into the Presence of God. It is the moment when the lover and the beloved unite. As you arrive at the top of the pyramid, you discover that you are the beautiful radiant pyramid and that God has always been at the apex of your soul.

The moment of my soul's sweet surrender occurred in an instant, it seems, but a long period of preparation had preceded it. Through meditation, prayer, purification, forgiveness, healing, I ventured further and further out into the realities that transcended the senses and obviated the ego. There was a complete transition from the life of the senses to the life of spirit. The surrender occurred and I was empty, caught in a void of nothingness.

Then, one night I woke up from a deep sleep with a fire raging up my spine. Intense heat coursed through my whole body and there was pressure in the back of my head. The fire stopped at my heart for a few moments and then continued ascending to the energy center at the top of my head. This energy center opened so wide, it seemed to have no beginning and no end. The top of my head was blazing, but there was something reassuring about the heat. A channel of the purest Light opened at the top of my head and I felt myself rushing out through the channel of Light. As I journeyed upward, the speed at which I traveled increased. My surroundings became lighter and brighter. I came to rest at a void somewhere beyond the stars and I was aware that the stars had not been born yet. I rested there blissfully, like an infant in a womb. Although the void was infinite, boundless, I felt at peace Then, at a distance, I saw a rim of light and knew that there was something else beyond the void or as part of the void. I was taken there and it was a beautiful Kingdom of Light. Everything was so beautiful and there were many beings of light. There were some beings I recognized from Earth.

I stood in front of rows of golden-edged books in what looked like a vast and ancient library. Then I floated higher and found myself in front of four of what seemed like very high beings of Light sitting behind a long table. There were four signs with golden letters suspended in the air above each of the beings. The signs read: WISDOM, JUSTICE, PEACE and LOVE. These beings directed energy to my heart and told me that everything I needed was in my heart; to go and do what I was meant to do. I thanked them and began rising even higher until I was somewhere else, a beautiful place flooded with radiant light. A unicorn appeared and I rode on its back to many beautiful places. I was shown countless dimensions, all very different. Some were made of ruby-colored stone, others were green and lush like tropical forests, some were just light. I was also taken to a very dark place with much pain and suffering. I was given a revelation about this place of darkness.

When I returned to my physical environment, the energy center at the top of my head was very hot and immense. Then, I felt my heart. It was incredible! It was so spacious and luminous. I felt that my whole being was in my heart, that my heart contained me and all existence. It was vast and beautiful beyond words and it took over everything. My heart was one with the Creator and within the Creator was all existence. At that moment when the Oneness with All-That-Is was so strong, a rush of understanding and realizations that exist beyond words flooded my being. Every cell in my body, every atom was saturated with a knowingness that was fresh and new, alive and awake. I have attempted to put the revelations into words, but the Divine Light that underlies the Truth goes far beyond words. It endows us with a Love that has no conditions, no boundaries. It is a gift from our Creator that is meant to be fluid, evolving and vibrant.

After that night, I had many profound mystical experiences. I received numerous attunements, initiations and empowerments from the spiritual realms to help me integrate and bring to the physical world the experience of union. I also received inner teachings to help me understand my visions.

As I became entwined with the Light, I was overwhelmed with gratitude at the enormity of this gift of unconditional Love and bliss. I am grateful to have been blessed with the beauty of the Light. I am grateful for the Light of the Creator's Love. I am grateful for all the beings of Light who assist me. I am grateful to our beloved Creator for guiding me every moment and giving me this opportunity to awaken to divine Love. I am grateful for the task given to me to share what I have experienced.

Now, in the moment when I exist, there is a stillness in my heart that like an undisturbed lake is clear and silent. Nothing moves it. My heart simply is. Beyond joy, beyond love, beyond yearning, beyond caring, there is the stillness of being that has no name, for it is beyond names. It has no goal for it is beyond that. It is an imperturbable beingness.

Here is what I was given to share with you: The Love of the Creator contains within Itself all of existence. It embraces all things within Itself, within Its Light. If you look for the Creator outside of yourself, you will never find him. You find the Creator by not looking. You can only know the Creator when you have let go of your idea of who he is.

All existence depends on the Creator. The Creator is not a being. The Creator is being Itself. There is nothing that is not the Creator. The Creator Is All. Your whole being is contained within the Creator's being. You have always existed in the Creator. You are eternal.

All Creation is an act of Love. So it follows that everything done with love is more precious. As you cook, drive, work and do so with love in your heart, you align to divine Love, the most powerful energy in the universe. You align to the Creator who is Love.

The Path of Light is one of devotion to the Creator. It is a journey where you realize who you truly are: a divine being who is a spark of the Creator. Love of God becomes all-encompassing. You love God and only God and your path becomes a path of Love. Love of God is the only love you are capable of feeling. Your love of God overflows from your heart and touches everything and everyone in existence. You no longer love God in others. You love only God and love others in God.

Love is complete dedication to the Creator, relinquishing our personal desires to his will and surrendering our lives to him. Love is the focused movement of our hearts toward the Creator. Love of God is our source of joy. We love everything and everyone in God. Everything we do is fueled by our love and devotion to God. Love is the secret of the universe. When we have known true Love, when we have loved this way, there is nothing else to know, nothing else to seek. Everything has been given to us and, once we find it, all we want is to rest in God's heart.

Once you are one with God, you are conscious not just that the presence of God is in you, but that the presence of God is in everyone you see. Each person is the Presence of God appearing to you in time, space and matter. In the state of union you fulfill the purpose of life, which is to know God. Once you know God, you let him express himself through you.

The Creator becomes everything. If the Creator is not everything, you end up seeking, searching for the divine in special places, distinctive activities, following methods that will not bear fruit because you lose yourself in thinking, in seeking, in searching. When you are in the state of union, you are never content with anything less than the Creator. To attain union you must desire only the Creator, love only the Creator and love all things in him.

When the Creator becomes your all, your life is lighted by divine radiance. Everything in your life reflects that Light. For this you must see all things in the Creator, acknowledge the Creator's presence in all others. Every time you look in someone's eyes, you see the Creator there. The Creator is the infinite ocean of being and we are drops in the ocean. Every person is a spark of the Creator, a divine child. And you are every person's family.

Sit quietly and rest in your heart. The Creator is always there. The Kingdom of God is within you. You must remember to sustain God-awareness, God-consciousness in everything you do. Once you are aware, conscious at all times of the Creator's presence within, that you are One with the Divine Presence, once you surrender everything to the Creator; a Light ignites in your heart, the Light of the Creator's Love, and you begin to radiate this Love, this Light to all.

When you are in union, you always remember the Creator and forget yourself, since nothing is yours to give or to accept, even your will is not your own, it is the Creator's. As you forget yourself, you rest in the nothingness of just being, still and quiet in the breath of God.

In the radiant chamber of union at the apex of the pyramid, there is much silence. You might not hear sounds or voices. The visions and revelations you may have experienced in previous stages of the path will be fewer and have a different quality. You might experience, as I have, that the Creator imprints the knowledge you need to have in the deepest part of your being. It is always there, like a treasure to be mined as needed. You realize that you have an understanding you did not have before. Another vista opens up before you and without having to see anything or hear anything, the realization is there. And you know that it is the truth, you have a spiritual certitude that what you know comes from the highest plane of Light and the knowledge is unwavering and unassailable.

This reminds me of Buddha who experienced his enlightenment and the revelations he received with absolute certainty. When Buddha reached enlightenment many spiritual teachers came to him and asked, "How do you know you are enlightened?" "You were alone when this happened, so who can witness it? Where is the proof?" Buddha, sitting under the bodhi tree where he had reached oneness, simply placed his hand on the ground and said: "The Earth is my witness."

It is common at this stage that though the visions and revelations are less common and sometimes stop altogether, the knowledge that is imprinted on the soul comes through with absolute certainty. The knowingness has a power, an authority that prevents any doubt from creeping in. You are certain that what you know is the Truth. The conviction is deep within you of the Truth that has been conveyed to your soul and there is no doubt, there is no fear. On the contrary there is a deep, abiding peace in the center of your being. At the same time you feel the power of the understanding, whether it has come through in words, visions or knowingness. Certainty, power, trust, and a profound peace are the signs of a true spiritual revelation.

Once you attain union with God, even the most mundane activity becomes divine, as the following experience I had while cooking one evening.

I am peeling garlic cloves and an onion. As I peel, I am deeply aware of the sound of the knife as it slices the tip of the garlic clove and the pungent scent that rises as I peel the cloves. While being aware of all the sensations, including the slight tingle on the skin at the edge of my fingernails, I am aware of the gentle hum of the refrigerator and the presence of my two cats, Frida and Diego, who are napping in another room. Though they are napping, I know with absolute certainty that at that moment of "no time" they are conscious of the sounds coming from the kitchen and of my movements.

When I finish peeling the garlic cloves and the onion, I observe the beautiful tableau on the wooden cutting board. I am aware of the pearly translucence of the cloves and the feathery texture of the onion skin. I feel the roundness of the onion in my own body and am aware of the layers of skin that I too am blessed with. As I look at the onion, garlic, cutting board, aware of all without any need for thought, I am also aware of the Divine Presence in my whole being which at that moment of no time is now One with the onion, the garlic, the cutting board, the cats, infinity and eternity. I know I rest gently in the Hand of God.

God-consciousness, awareness of the Creator's presence within you, is the blessing that awakens you and brings you to the true reality of your being. Once you know this, there is no further need for learning anything, for praying, for listening to teachings, for reading spiritual books, for seeking anything anywhere. Once this awareness is there and you are awakened to the reality of God's presence, you are fully in the Realm of Light, in God's Kingdom. You are One with God, One with All-That-Is.

You attain this realization when your heart is so full of the Creator that nothing else can enter it. There is no place for joy or sadness, for suffering or contentment, for desire or fear or longing. Nothing else can exist in your heart, only the Creator. You are there, in the Creator, sitting with him at his throne of Light.

In this divine place of perfection and Love, there is no anger, or sorrow, or disappointment, or fear. There is only the Creator and your union with the Creator. Your self dissolves in God and spirals away, in union, into infinity, like a figure 8, going on and on, without beginning or end. From that exalted state of being, you become the instrument through whom God brings his Love into the world.

Nothing can be added to or subtracted from the One. The Creator is and everything else is nothing. When you are in pure union with the Creator, you abide in the nothingness of existence where only the Creator is.

There are no divisions; nothing is separate. You rest in the wholeness of the Creator alone.

In the moment of union, all your life becomes being. You are dead to self and alive to God. You have ceased to be. And you realize that in the true Reality of God's Love you never needed to be united to him. You were always one with the Beloved.

So let the Creator be in you and work his magnificence through you. Union with God is surrendering completely to his will. Let go of your concept of the Creator and get out of his way. Once you let go of your idea of the Creator, your wanting things from the Creator, your clinging to the desires and attachments of the ego, when you have let your ego dissolve and forgotten yourself, the veil between you and the Creator dissolves and what remains is the One. In this union with the Creator, you are reborn as the divine child within the sacred space of your heart. You are reborn into the Light in a sacred birthing that makes you whole and complete and perfect. And you are free, fully awakened to your true nature.

At this eternal, infinite instant when all is still and time collapses into the moment, you find that you no longer need to pray, nor ask another to pray for you. You reach a stage where you do nothing. You do not love, nor work, nor know, nor learn because the Creator does everything through you. The Creator loves and works and knows through you. You become a perfect instrument of his Light.

In union you are aware that the Realm of Light is inside you, right there in the sacred space of your heart. God's Throne is in your heart and there he sits in all his glory. Your rebirth as a divine child depends on one thing and one thing only: your awareness of it. When the Creator begets the divine child in you and you are reborn, you transcend the limitations of time, space and matter, you surrender everything you are and you reach the Grace of his presence. Enlightenment unfolds in your heart. You are pure. You are One with God.

Epilogue

There was once a very ancient kingdom ruled by a benevolent monarch. One day, the king asked one of his trusted subjects to travel to a faraway forest and find a hidden chest that contained scrolls with important messages. These writings would ensure the survival of the kingdom. The king gave his subject specific instructions on where to find the chest and he told him that the chest had to be brought back as soon as possible. Otherwise, the kingdom would be in grave danger of extinction.

The man set off on his journey with a bounce in his step, proud that the king had given him such a meaningful task. But before he reached his destination, he ran into a beggar. He decided that it would be a good thing to stop and help this needy person. Many days went by while the man sought food and clothing for the beggar. Once he was sure that the needy man had a source of food and clothing, he continued his journey.

A few days afterwards, the man hurried along a trail of isolated cottages. A slight breeze carried the smell of burnt wood and when he looked up at the sky he saw ashes whirling above him. He rushed ahead and saw the remains of a house that had burnt down. A despondent family stared at the piles of embers and ashes and the children wept. The man immediately offered his assistance and spent many weeks helping the family rebuild their house. And so it was throughout the journey. A long time passed and the man became so distracted with all the "good" deeds he was doing that he completely forgot the important mission given to him by the king. The kingdom perished.

It would be wise to avoid the error of the man in our story. Our destiny of Light is to return to the Creator, to unite with his Light so that we may reflect this Light to the world. Yet, often we are too distracted doing things that seem to be quite good, but that only serve as a diversion so that we do not fulfill our true purpose. This is the function of the ego: to distract us sufficiently so that we avoid fulfilling our soul's purpose.

We have not come to this world to accomplish all the things that we are bent on doing. We have come to reach union with the Creator and to be his instrument of Light in a world that needs it so much. Being an instrument of Light is much more significant than doing the logical things our mind convinces us we must do if we are to help others and ourselves.

The Path of Light that the Creator has shown me and that I describe as a luminous pyramid, will help you to fulfill your mission of Light. The five stages of the Path toward union with the Creator are not rigid. They flow gently one into the other. You can ascend the spiral staircase with a light and happy heart, since this Path offers you boundless joy. As you enter the radiant quartz pyramid with a joyful heart, you will realize that this ascent toward the apex is a journey through beautiful landscapes, offering blessings at every step. The Path provides the necessary rest so you can catch your breath whenever you need a respite before continuing your rise up the stairs. Although our spiritual path must be undertaken with the seriousness it deserves, it is also important not to rush so much that the path becomes an unpleasant obsession rather than a wondrous pilgrimage to the Creator's sweet embrace.

If at any time you harbor doubts about the discipline or the teacher or the spiritual practice you follow to reach union with the Creator, always remember that a genuine path is one that will bring you to an awareness of God's presence within yourself. Follow the path that guides you toward the Creator's presence in your heart, that helps you to feel his Love and that offers you opportunities to be the Creator's instrument by being of service to others. If a spiritual practice promises powers or states of ecstasy that do not bring you to God-consciousness, it is best not to follow it. Stay firm in the understanding that the only power is in the Creator and the Creator is All.

We are the Creator's divine children. We are reborn in the Light every moment and, at the same time, we have always existed in the Beloved's Heart. Remember always: you walk in the Light.

About the Author

Since she experienced a spiritual transformation many years ago, the mystic Alba Ambert has been an instrument of the Creator bringing a reminder of Love and Light. She received the Paramita Path, a system of spiritual healing and growth leading to enlightenment, as a result of deep mystical experiences. Since then, she is dedicated to transmitting the teachings of the Paramita Path internationally. She has a doctorate in psycholinguistics from Harvard. She is a published novelist, poet, essayist, short story writer and author of children's books. She has also authored *The Seven Powers of Spiritual Evolution, Your Sacred Space: A Guide to a Light-Filled Home, Your Sacred Apothecary* and *The Paramita Path To Healing and Spiritual Growth.*

About the Paramita Path

Paramita Path workshops are offered in the U.S., Latin America and Europe. A brief description of some of our workshops follows. For complete information on our programs, please visit: www.paramitapath.org

Paramita Path Foundation

You develop the ability to channel Divine Light for self-healing and to heal others. Your energy channels are prepared to awaken your Kundalini on the second day of the workshop. You are synchronized with the elemental energies (Air, Fire, Water, Earth and Spirit) to activate these in your energy channels so that you can use elemental energies for healing and spiritual growth. You start the process of opening your heart and connecting, through your heart, to the Love of the Creator. Your chakras, sushumna and energy channels are cleared and opened to be able to radiate Divine Light for healing and spiritual purposes. You learn to do self-healing and to heal others. You learn to scan and balance your chakras. You receive specific lessons related to the Paramitas, the path to enlightenment based on unconditional love and compassion. Through special meditations, you begin to feel unconditional love for all beings and you embark on the beautiful path of the Bodhisattva.

You receive three lotuses for your heart, ajna and crown chakras to help you open your heart to the Divine Love and Light, to assist you in perceiving the subtle reality more effectively and to assist you to open your spiritual center and connect better to the divine energies. You also receive the spiritual wings you will need to complete your mission of unconditional love and service to humanity. Your Kundalini is awakened and you begin a process of spiritual purification. You learn more about the Paramitas to help you live as an evolved being. You learn advanced techniques for healing, including distant healing. You learn techniques to protect yourself from negative energies. You learn meditations to fill you with Love and Light and radiate it to others. You become a beautiful beacon of Light.

Paramita Path Expansion

You begin an accelerated process of spiritual growth with special attunements, meditations and practices specifically designed to place you firmly on a path directed towards enlightenment through Divine Love and unconditional love for all beings. Five additional chakras are opened and activated and you learn advanced healing techniques. You deepen your understanding of the Paramitas, the practices of love and compassion that assist you in your spiritual path. You learn techniques to break free of the attachments that are an obstacle to spiritual growth. You learn to radiate unconditional love to any situation or person and change your reality by working with the Light.

Healing Your Karma

You learn a powerful process to heal your karma in relationships, situations, behaviors, physical and spiritual conditions. This process will assist you in removing karmic obstacles that prevent the full flowering of your spirit as your soul regains the absolute purity of the Light.

Awakening Your Heart

In this workshop you open and awaken your spiritual heart for accelerated spiritual growth. Through specially designed attunements, empowerments, meditations and practices, you awaken your heart and connect with your soul and spirit. This constitutes great progress in your journey toward enlightenment.

You learn a beautiful technique to ask guidance from your heart. You learn to radiate unconditional love more effectively allowing you to be a true beacon of Love and Light. As you open your heart and access the Sacred Space of your heart, you can listen to the wisdom of your True Self while you connect completely with the Creator's Heart. This places you firmly on the path leading to enlightenment through Divine Love and unconditional love toward all beings.

You learn techniques that free you from the attachments that are an obstacle to opening your heart and you come to a deep understanding of the ego and the necessity to dissolve it. A special meditation you can add to your spiritual practice clears your mind and subsconscious and dissolves emotions and unnecessary thoughts. You learn to radiate unconditional love to any situation or person and to change your reality by working with the Light in your heart.

At this advanced level you begin to remember who you really are, beyond your physical and personal identity. At this level of Light you acquire the consciousness that you are a divine being, a being of Light.

In addition to the material described above, you receive spiritual teachings that are only transmitted orally.

Dissolving Your Ego

A crucial step in attaining Oneness with the Creator is the dissolution of your ego. In this workshop you learn to identify the behaviors, traits and fixed beliefs that are ego-based and you learn powerful and effective steps to let them go. You acquaint yourself with the shadow self and learn specific techniques to bring it to the light for self-awareness and spiritual growth.

Creating Your Sacred Space

In this workshop you learn to identify and remove unbalanced energies from your home, workplace and any other space and fill them with Light. Using simple exercises and a variety of practices, you can transform your space into a beacon of Light that affects the outside world. You learn to distinguish between a variety of unbalanced energies and learn effective techniques to clear each of these. You discover how to bring harmony to your living and work spaces. You also learn the most effective way to cure geopathic stress to bring healing and balance into your space. By following the methods discussed in the workshop, you can transform your space into an oasis of radiant light bringing harmony, comfort and serenity to all who live there and to your environment.

The Path Of Your Soul

In all your reincarnations you have lived the experiences that have helped you grow spiritually. You may have wondered: "What has happened in past lives?" "What happens between reincarnations?" "What are the lessons I came to learn in my present life?" "How did the cycle of reincarnation begin?" "Why did we separate from the Creator?" In this workshop you will learn many of the mysteries of your soul's progress and learn techniques to find answers to specific questions regarding the path of your soul. Through meditations, practices and regressions you will gain soul consciousness and attain a deeper understanding of why you are here.

Paramita Path Centers

United States
Paramita Path Center
North Carolina, U.S.A.
Telephone: 919 338-7818
Email: mail@paramitapath.org
Website: www.paramitapath.org

Puerto Rico
Centro de Sendero Paramita
San Juan, Puerto Rico
Telephone: 787 646-3591
Email: info@senderoparamita.org
Website: www.senderoparamita.org

Spain
Paramita Path at La Calma
Centro Wellness La Calma
Ribadesella, Asturias, Spain
Telephone: +34 985 861 804
Email: info@la-calma.es
Website: www.la-calma.es
(Programs at La Calma are run in both Spanish and English)